Brownstone M ☐ **Y0-ABH-680**

ISSN 1055-6859

Volume Twelve

Hard-Boiled Heretic

*The
Lew Archer
Novels
of
Ross Macdonald*

by

Mary S. Weinkauf

Edited by Mary Wickizer Burgess

Brownstone Books
SAN BERNARDINO, CALIFORNIA
Distributed by THE BORGO PRESS
Nineteen Ninety-Four

THE BORGO PRESS
Publishers Since 1975
Post Office Box 2845
San Bernardino, CA 92406
United States of America

*   *   *   *   *   *   *   *

Library of Congress Cataloging-in-Publication Data

Weinkauf, Mary S. (Mary Stanley), 1938-
  Hard-boiled heretic : the Lew Archer novels of Ross Macdonald / by
Mary S. Weinkauf ; edited by Mary A. Burgess.
    p. cm. (Brownstone mystery guides, ISSN 1055-6859 ; v. 12)
  Includes bibliographical references and index.
  ISBN 0-89370-172-6 (cloth). — ISBN 0-89370-272-2 (pbk.)
  1. Macdonald, Ross, 1915- —Characters—Lew Archer. 2. Detective and
mystery stories, American—History and criticism. 3. Archer, Lew (Ficti-
tious character) 4. California in literature. 5. Detectives in literature. I.
Burgess, Mary Wickizer, 1938- . II. Title. III. Series.
PS3525.I486Z92 1994
813'.52—dc19   84-282
                                                                      CIP

FIRST EDITION

CONTENTS

ABOUT THE AUTHOR

MARY S. WEINKAUF is currently pastor of the Siloa/Faith Lutheran Parish (Evangelical Lutheran Church in America), Ontonagon and White Pine, in Michigan's Upper Peninsula. Before entering Lutheran School of Theology at Chicago for her Master of Divinity degree, she taught at the University of Tennessee (where she received her doctorate in 1966), Adrian College, and Dakota Wesleyan University (as head of the English department and chairman of the Humanities division, 1969-89).

Reverend Weinkauf has published articles in *Studies in English Literature*, *Extrapolation*, *Riverside Quarterly*, *Midwest Review*, *Clues*, and other scholarly periodicals, as well as numerous reviews, poems, news articles, and short stories. She is the author of book-length critiques of Ngaio Marsh and S. Fowler Wright (forthcoming from Borgo Press).

She was ordained in May, 1993, but keeps her detective fiction with her Bible commentaries.

CHRONOLOGY

1915 Kenneth Millar [i.e., Ross Macdonald] is born in Los Gatos, California on December 13, 1915, the son of Canadian citizens, John Macdonald and Ann Millar. The family moves to Vancouver, where John Millar plies his trade as a harbor pilot, but considers himself a journalist and poet. Kenneth spends his childhood playing with the children of Japanese fishermen, and developing his life-long love of the ocean.

1919 Millar recalls "a brief voyage with his sea-captain father." Following WWI, his parents separate, and Kenneth's mother takes him to her home territory in Ontario, where "from then on I lived mostly with her and her people." Begins to write verse and fiction before the age of twelve. Reads *Oliver Twist* by Charles Dickens which leaves a lifelong impression on him, as does *Huckleberry Finn* by Mark Twain, and the work of Stephen Crane.

1921 Macdonald's mother, without resources of her own, prepares to place him in an orphanage. His father's cousin, Rob Millar, takes him instead. The young Kenneth becomes hooked on the "cliff-hanger" serials, such as "Pearl White," shown at Rob Millar's movie theatre in Wiarton, Ontario.

1926 For two years Kenneth attends St. John's, a private boarding school in Winnipeg; his tuition is paid by his father's younger sister, Margaret. He spends his spare time writing a "sheaf of Western stories and a long narrative poem about Bonnie Prince Charlie," and gains an insight into how "more prosperous" families live.

1929 Discovers "Falcon Swift the Monocled Manhunter," a fictional detective regularly featured in the *Boys' Magazine*. The Stock Market crash "propels" him out of boarding school, and further West, where he spends most of his teen years "with relatives and friends in over fifty different houses."

1931 Returns to his family's original home in Ontario, and lives with his mother in her mother's house in Kitchener while attending high school. His first published story, "The South Sea Soup Co.," a parody of Conan Doyle, appears in the Kitchener Collegiate Institute *Grumbler*. His future wife, Margaret Sturm's first story, "Impromptu," appears there also. Yearbook pictures confirm they are on the school debating team together, although they don't begin dating for several more years. Kenneth graduates from high school, and leaves home to work on a farm for a year.

1936   Begins college, but drops out of school briefly to travel in Europe, where he spends two revealing months in Nazi Germany.

1938   Kenneth Millar and Margaret "Maggie" Sturm are married in June, the day after he is graduated from the University of Western Ontario with honors. They honeymoon in Ann Arbor. In the fall they move to the University of Toronto, where Kenneth prepares to become a high school teacher.

1939   Millar's daughter Linda (now deceased) is born. He goes to hear Lord Tweedsmuir (i.e., John Buchan, author of *The Thirty-Nine Steps*) give a high school graduation address. He wins a typewriter on a radio quiz show, and begins writing professionally for the Toronto *Saturday Night*. Margaret begins to write mystery novels.

1941   Margaret's literary success, beginning with the first of her "Paul Prye" novels, *The Invisible Worm*, enables Kenneth to leave off teaching high school in Kitchener and accept a full-time fellowship at the University of Michigan in Ann Arbor. The Millars move to the United States for good.

1943   Kenneth writes his first novel, *The Dark Tunnel*, in Ann Arbor. It is based on his experiences in pre-War Nazi Germany, and is influenced by the work of John Buchan. He is accepted at Officers Candidate School at Princeton.

1944   *The Dark Tunnel* is published by Dodd, Mead. Millar becomes an ensign in the U.S. Naval Reserve.

1945   His story, "Find the Woman" (originally titled "Death by Water") is written aboard the U.S.S. *Shipley Bay*, an escort carrier "somewhere between San Francisco and Kwajalein." On the advice of Anthony Boucher, he enters the story in an Ellery Queen contest and it wins a $400 prize. Margaret Millar, living in Hollywood during the war, begins working for Warner Brothers, writing a screenplay for "The Iron Gates."

1946   Millar is discharged from the Navy with the rank of Lt. (j.g.), in March, and rejoins his wife and daughter in California. *Trouble Follows Me* is published by Dodd, Mead. Writes *Blue City*, and his first "California" novel, *The Three Roads*.

1947   Millar begins using the pseudonyms "John Macdonald" and "John Ross Macdonald" on a regular basis. The names are derived from his father's name, and his Scottish-Canadian forebears. He begins penning the first three "Lew Archer" titles, starting with *The Moving Target*, loosely patterned after Raymond Chandler's "Philip Marlowe" stories. He uses his sister-in-law Dorothy Schlagel's Hollywood apartment for writing while she is away at work during the day.

1949   *The Moving Target* is published by Alfred Knopf, the publisher of Hammett and Chandler.

1950   *The Drowning Pool* is published by Knopf

1951   Receives his Ph.D. in English from the University of Michigan. *The Way Some People Die* is published.

1952   Publishes *The Ivory Grin.*

1953   Moves to the Bay area for a year, settling not far from his birthplace in Los Gatos. *Meet Me at the Morgue* is published by Knopf. *The Ivory Grin* is reissued as *Marked for Murder* by Pocket Books.

1954   Publishes *Find a Victim.*

1955   Begins writing his longest book thus far, *The Barbarous Coast*. One of the characters, George Wall, is an "angry young Canadian lost in Hollywood." His story collection, *The Name is Archer*, is published by Bantam.

1956   Knopf publishes *The Barbarous Coast*. Margaret Millar's novel, *Beast in View*, wins the Edgar Allen Poe award.

1957   Takes a summer house in Santa Barbara where he becomes acquainted with the English poet Donald Davie. Begins work on his semi-autobiographical "break-through" novel, *The Galton Case.*

1958   *The Doomsters* is published.

1959   *The Galton Case* is published.

1960   *The Ferguson Affair* is published.

1961   *The Wycherly Woman* is published.

1962   One of Millar's own favorites, *The Zebra-Striped Hearse*, is published.

1964   The Coyote Canyon forest fire threatens Santa Barbara and its environs. *The Chill* is published.

1965   Receives the Crime Writers Association Silver Dagger Award. *The Far Side of the Dollar* is published.

1966   *Black Money*, another personal favorite, is published. *The Moving Target* is filmed by Warner Brothers, as *Harper*, starring Paul Newman in the title role. (Newman insists that the detective's name be changed from "Archer" to "Harper" because of a superstition he has regarding the letter "H.")

1968   *The Instant Enemy* is published.

1969   An oil well on Union Platform A off the coast of Santa Barbara erupts causing a disastrous oil spill. Kenneth and Margaret Millar, already enthusiastic environmentalists and bird-lovers, become even more actively involved in the subsequent ecological uproar, and these concerns continue to have a lasting influence on their writing. *The Goodbye Look* is published.

1971   *The Underground Man*, featuring a devastating forest fire similar to the Coyote Canyon fire as a unifying theme, is published.

1972   Receives the University of Michigan Outstanding Achievement Award.

1973   Receives the Mystery Writers of America Grand Master Award, and the Popular Culture Association Award of Excellence. Publishes *Sleeping Beauty*, which takes its theme from the earlier disastrous Santa Barbara oil spill. *On Crime Writing*, a collection of Millar's non-fiction essays, is published by Capra Press, a Santa Barbara fine press publisher. He meets Ralph B. Sipper, a local specialty book-dealer.

1974 *Great Stories of Suspense*, an anthology edited by Millar, is published by Knopf. *The Underground Man* is filmed for television, and stars Peter Graves as Lew Archer.

1975 A PBS television documentary of Millar's life is filmed at his request in the bookstore belonging to his friend, Ralph Sipper.

1976 *The Blue Hammer* is published, and reflects Millar's concerns with the themes of urban and social decay. *The Drowning Pool* is filmed as a sequel to *Harper*, and also stars Paul Newman in the title role. His wife, Joanne Woodward, joins him, as does Melanie Griffith, who plays Woodward's Lolita-type daughter.

1977 A collection of short stories, *Lew Archer: Private Investigator*, is published by Mysterious Press.

1979 *A Collection of Reviews* is published by Lord John Press.

1981 Receives the Private Eye Writers of America Life Achievement Award. *Self-Portrait: Ceaselessly into The Past*, a collection of autobiographical essays, is published by Capra Press. (The sub-title is a quotation from *The Great Gatsby*, by F. Scott Fitzgerald, one of Macdonald's idols.)

1982 *Self-Portrait* wins the *Los Angeles Times* Robert Kirsch Award.

1983 Margaret Millar, now legally blind, receives her second Edgar for *Banshee*, as well as the Grand Master Award from Mystery Writers of America. Ross Macdonald [Kenneth Millar] dies of Alzheimer's disease on July 11, 1983.

1994 Margaret Millar dies on March 29.

A CRITIC'S VIEW

Perhaps the single quality linking the work of husband and wife, beyond the setting of Southern California and the detection story form, is their clear and copious compassion for their imagined characters as tokens...for real-life figures caught in somewhat comparable dramas that are neither imaginary nor satisfactorily soluble.

—Charles Champlin
The Los Angeles Times

I.

THE "HARD-BOILED" HERETIC

*But down these mean streets a man must go who is not
himself mean, who is neither tarnished nor afraid.*

—Raymond Chandler,
The Simple Art of Murder

"The hardest of the hard-boiled dicks" is how the paperback publishers have described Ross Macdonald's Lew Archer. In reality, though, Archer is much more dedicated and caring than some tough, aloof loner who rises from a beating and jogs ten miles to the nearest bar to recuperate. Even Archer himself uses the phrase "unfrocked priest" to describe himself in *The Drowning Pool*, a surprisingly appropriate epithet.

Lew Archer is a twentieth-century Renaissance man who reflects the interests and problems of his time. He is knowledgeable in art, literature, music, and psychology. Against the backdrop of the broken lives and abandoned dreams of others he suffers the pain of his own divorce and scuttled police career. He moves easily, like a chameleon, from the murky world of the illegal alien to the shining mansions of California's first families. Wherever he goes he is at home and trusted by saint and sinner alike. Through it all his priestly qualities endow him with the ability—and the need—to touch the lives of the people he encounters. He is both a comforter and a healer let loose in a less than ideal world.

"Private eye" is a metaphor, not only for a hired voyeur who peeps through keyholes and windows, but also (in Archer's case) for an observant problem-solver. Archer gazes into people's souls and learns not just *who* they are, but *why* they do some of the things they do. He uncovers not only the killer but the motive as well, even if he must trace through generations and, sometimes literally, dig up old skeletons to explain new corpses. He follows the truth wherever it may lead him. The only fear he ever admits to is that of being blinded, of being unable to see—of being unable to discern the truth.

11

The private eye is both a modern occupation and a modern literary preoccupation. The literary pathway leading from C. Auguste Dupin and Sherlock Holmes to Spade and Marlowe closely parallels fiction's transition from romance to realism. Holmes and Dupin were gentlemen amateurs, with only their reputations to lose. The twentieth century private eye, however, is first and foremost a businessman, with a license, an office, and a livelihood riding on how well he copes with a sometimes mundane, if necessary, job. Sherlock Holmes used logic as his primary tool for getting at the truth. While reason and painstaking observations still play a large part in crime-solving, new scientific devices have also found a place in the modern-day sleuth's arsenal.

To a detective like Lew Archer, however, the physical evidence is still far less important than his own intuitive skills and use of human psychology. This modern fictional detective probes the subconscious minds of criminal and victim alike. He is a master psychologist—with a license to practice detection.

Lew Archer's predecessors in the hard-boiled tradition are clearly Sam Spade and Philip Marlowe. (Sherlock Holmes is so far removed from the hard-boiled detective, however, that when Archer identifies himself as "Holmes, S." in *The Zebra-Striped Hearse*, it is cynically, with tongue firmly in cheek). Spade and Marlowe are tough and street-wise, but both have a limited interest in intellectual matters. Neither makes much money, but neither seems to value financial success as much as they value moral victories. Neither could be categorized as "saintly." Spade has been sleeping with his partner Miles Archer's wife and cares little for police regulations or the strict letter of the law, while Marlowe is ruthless and disillusioned by the corruption he sees around him. Both men lead violent lives and often seek violent solutions to the moral dilemmas they are forced to confront.

The modern private eye genre reveals a great deal about the profession of detection. Organized police and professional private detectives are relative newcomers to the work force. Pinkerton's National Police Agency was founded just before the Civil War and developed in Chicago, a city that grew too fast for its politically-appointed police to manage.

Among Pinkerton's twentieth century operatives was Dashiell Hammett, who was hired at the tender age of twenty-two after a string of temporary jobs. "Sam" Hammett worked undercover as a member of the I.W.W., picking up a few scars and a great deal of practical experience along the way. He did well, eventually moving to Pinkerton's San Francisco office after World War I, although he was forced to resign in 1922 because of tuberculosis (after only 2½ years as an actual operative).

Hammett had a chance to see a world most of his contemporaries never glimpsed. The stories derived from his experiences bear little resemblance to the genteel tales of sleuths and criminals of earlier detective works, or even the adventures of contemporary gentleman detectives like Philo Vance. In *The Simple Art of Murder*, Raymond Chandler praised Hammett's talent for putting crime into the real world where people speak the actual language of criminals. Sam Spade, the detective who walked alone through "these mean streets," was immortalized in *The Continental Op* as a hero who invented a new direction for the realistic private eye. (Hammett's other popular creations, Nick and Nora Charles, were wealthy socialites facing real criminal situations, a further departure from standard detective fiction.)

The next link in Archer's literary lineage is Raymond Chandler's Philip Marlowe. In *Mortal Consequences*, Julian Symons refers to Archer as "something near to a carbon copy" of Marlowe. It would have been difficult for Macdonald to avoid being influenced by Chandler. Marlowe is the epitomé of the hard-boiled detective—cynical, tough, battered, smart-mouthed, worldly-wise, lower class, free of ties, brave, and utterly dedicated to finding the truth. Capable of withstanding enormous physical abuse and accustomed to seeing the worst in people, Marlowe still manages to retain a semblance of his idealism. Chandler's detective is graphically depicted in this now-famous passage from "The Simple Art of Murder":

> But down these mean streets a man must go who is not himself mean, who is neither tarnished nor afraid. The detective in this kind of story must be such a man. He is the hero; he is everything. He must be a complete man and a common man and yet an unusual man. He must be, to use a rather weathered phrase, a man of honor—by instinct, by inevitability, without thought of it, and certainly without saying it. He must be the best man in his world and a good enough man for any world. I do not care much about his private life; he is neither a eunuch nor a satyr; I think he might seduce a duchess and I am quite sure he would not spoil a virgin; if he is a man of honor in one thing, he is that in all things.
>
> He is a relatively poor man, or he would not be a detective at all. He is a common man or he could not go among common people. He has a sense of character, or he would not know his job. He will take no man's money dishonestly and no man's insolence without a due and dispassionate revenge. He is a lonely man and his pride is that you will treat him as a proud man or be very sorry you ever saw him. He talks as the man of his age talks—that is, with rude wit, a lively sense of the grotesque, a disgust for sham, and a contempt for pettiness.[1]

He is, in other words, the modern equivalent of the knight er-rant. He mixes with crooked cops, corrupt politicians, sadistic gang-sters, and vicious beauties without being tarnished by their evil. Turn-ing down bribes, Marlowe makes his own way—he cannot be bought, only hired a day at a time. His only vices are smoking cigarettes and ingesting amazing quantities of alcohol. As Robert B. Parker has said of him:

> Marlowe is tough enough and brave enough to main-
> tain a system of values that is humanistic, romantic,
> sentimental, and chivalric. He is a man of honor.[2]

The lineage of the humanistic hard-boiled hero does not stop with Lew Archer. The scion of Philip Marlowe has himself spawned such descendents as Robert B. Parker's Spenser (who intentionally uses no first name). Spenser (who appears in *The Godwulf Manuscript, Promised Land, The Judas Goat, Mortal Stakes, God Save the Child,* and *Looking for Rachel Wallace,* among others, as well as the popular TV series) is a native Bostonian. Like his literary predecessors, he remains single, cocky, and smart-mouthed enough to aggravate client and suspect alike. He is intuitive, but not prosperous. Unlike Archer and Marlowe, he will sleep with female clients, although he eventually settles into a long-term relationship with Susan Silverman, a guidance counselor. Thus he is less lonely than the typical P.I. He works out at the Boston YMCA and gets the normal junk mail and bills of the average businessman. Like Archer he gets along well with young people. (The similarities to Archer, Marlowe, and Spade are not wholly surprising, in view of the fact that Parker's doctoral dissertation was *The Violent Hero, Wilderness Heritage and Urban Reality: A Study of the Private Eye in the Novels of Dashiell Hammett, Raymond Chan-dler and Ross Macdonald.*) Both Parker and Macdonald (Kenneth Millar) have Ph.D.s in literature rather than practical experience in police work, as did Hammett.

Spenser upholds the chivalric code of the hard-boiled detective and shares Archer's intense concern for the unity and health of the fam-ily. He is concerned as well with contemporary issues, such as femi-nism, gay rights, college radicals, professional baseball, runaways, and terrorism. Also, like Archer, Spenser continues to grow as a character, developing numerous interests and relationships peripheral to the mys-tery plots. He has become a solid member of the hard-boiled family. Parker has followed Macdonald, moreover, in breaking away from the "He is the hero; he is everything" pattern Chandler espoused. Archer and Spenser move among ordinary people who suffer extraordinary pain, helping them become whole again. In this respect, Archer and Spencer vary alike from the typical hard-boiled stereotype.

The private investigator fiction of Ross Macdonald has attracted increasing critical attention in the last decade. Several noteworthy studies have been published: Peter Wolfe's *Dreamers Who Live Their Dreams* (1976), and Jerry Speir's *Ross Macdonald* (1978), as well as Macdonald's own *Self-Portrait: Ceaselessly Into the Past* (Capra Press: 1981), a collection of autobiographical essays summarizing his life and work. He has secured (along with Dashiell Hammett and Raymond Chandler), a hard-won place beyond the usual mystery genre category as a seminal writer in the field of modern American literature.

QUALIFICATIONS FOR PRIVATE DETECTIVE

1. Honesty and loyalty
2. Capable of communicating ideals
3. Licensed by society
4. Humanistic education
5. Acceptance and devotion to law and order
6. Honest and law-abiding
7. Liable to lose license for infractions of law
8. Acts in accordance with laws of the state and human kindness
9. Cares for people as clients and as human beings
10. Teaches respect for society
11. Visits with young people
12. Stands up for law and order
13. Comforts victims and distressed
14. Solves past crimes (psychologically buries past burdens of guilt)
15. Encourages young to be useful
16. Passes on ideas
17. Keeps financial and case records

QUALIFICATIONS FOR LUTHERAN PASTOR

1. Soundness of faith
2. Aptness to teach
3. Ordained by God
4. Religious education
5. Acceptance & devotion to confession of faith
6. Life and conduct above reproach
7. Subject to recall
8. Acts in accordance with laws of the church and state
9. Cares for people individually and as a congregation
10. Gives instructions
11. Supervises schools and learning opportunities
12. Inculcates piety
13. Visits the sick
14. Buries the dead
15. Seeks and encourages young men and women to enter the ministry
16. Imparts knowledge
17. Keeps records

II.

A HUMANIST PRIEST
IN A SECULAR WORLD

He can be self-forgetful, almost transparent at times, and he concentrates as good detectives (and good writers) do, on the people whose problems he is investigating.

—Ross Macdonald,
"The Writer as Detective Hero"

In an interview with Sam Grogg, Jr. Ross Macdonald responded to a question about the centrality of murder in the detective story:

> It's the ultimate crime...in a secular society, and the mystery novel is essentially the expression of a secular society. But it's really symbolic. Murder stands for various kinds of crime. And, in fact, in my books it reflects other kinds of crime. It's the objective correlative, you might say, of spiritual death. That's why I write about extreme situations such as murder. They are a metaphor for our daily lives. We're close to the edge in many ways. Which is quite thrilling too. It's an interesting way to live, if you can survive it.[1]

Macdonald obviously felt that the detective genre was a useful format for writing about contemporary life. The hero of the detective novel is a narrator who serves as the eye of the author. He does not demand center stage, nor should he be too closely identified with his creator. And in fact, as Macdonald writes in the "Preface" to *The Galton Case*, Archer becomes practically invisible when he turns sideways!

Although Archer is very real to us, with specific personality traits, what Macdonald means here is that the other people in the story, its messages and motifs, are more important than the hero. We are not meant to marvel over Archer the way we do over Augustus S. F. X. Van Dusen, (The Thinking Machine). We are asked instead to empathize with the ordinary people with whom Archer comes in contact. Once Archer exorcizes the evil Puddler in *The Moving Target* (significantly he comes to regret this killing in later books), there are no further thorough-going villains. Even murderers and gangsters can arouse Archer's sympathy, and hence ours. Too many aspects of society can force people into violent actions, Archer implies, and we should not simple-mindedly class all criminals as "the bad guys."

Archer does not condemn. In fact, like Poirot, he allows a few of the crooks to go free, in hopes they will be rehabilitated. Miss Marple solves crimes by noting resemblances of a criminal to someone or some situation she once knew in her microcosm of an English village. Archer, on the other hand, sees something quite unique in each person he encounters. He has the ability to accept people as they are, recognizing even young people as individuals in a way few fictional detectives do. He is, in spite of his isolation, an open and caring individual, and very much a priestly character.

The phrase "humanist priest" may seem like a contradiction in terms, since the historic rites of the church—baptism, confirmation, matrimony, and extreme unction—are meaningless in secular terms. Yet, if the mystery novel is an expression of a secular society, who is the detective within the novel if not that society's representative? In his attempts to solve or prevent murder ("the objective correlative...of spiritual death"), he acts as a man with a mission to set things right, just as in the church, the clergy are responsible for seeing that the word of God is taught and the sacraments are administered properly.

The clergy is not an especially privileged group, but they *are* trained specialists who, as Arnold E. Carlson suggests, represent Christ and are God's ambassadors here on Earth. Another theologian, George W. Forell, says that the minister exists so that people can *come to faith.* Ultimately, the priest is responsible for providing continuity within the church. His responsibilities (see page 16, together with a job description for pastors of the Evangelical Lutheran Church in America), compare with surprising fidelity to the traits of Archer's behavior that mark him as special.

The detective ranges widely through his world, and is not limited to one particular dogma other than his moral code, which is often adhered to rigidly. He *is* worldly, and that experience forms part of his theology.

The roles of the priest and of the detective overlap, sometimes surprisingly, in several ways. The priest is set aside from the world, physically in some cases, and the detective, too, is a "loner," noted for his conscientious devotion to duty. Even though the detective operates in the secular world, he must be as dedicated to his code of ethics as the priest is to the moral code of the Church. However cynical the detective may become, he (like the priest) still maintains a core of hope for this world, and in like ways he serves as an agent for positive change. He fights against corruption, apathy, and evil, and at the end of each case someone is saved, spiritually if not physically, someone else is brought to justice, and a balance, however temporary, is restored to the world.

In *The World of the Thriller*, Ralph Harper suggests that the mystery novel has replaced *The Lives of the Saints* as popular reading material. The private eye has become the modern-day equivalent of St. George the dragon-slayer, who roamed the world to do battle with the forces of evil. The P.I.'s victories are all the more satisfying because they can be interpreted as the readers' victories as well. In this hard-boiled world, Casper Gutman, Joel Cairo and Professor Moriarity may be easier for the reader to handle psychologically than are real-life nemeses such as oil shortages, domestic squabbles, and street crime.

In *The Wounded Healer*, Henri J. Nouwen has analysed the role of the priest in relation to the problems of modern society, which, he feels, is filled with selfish, anti-authoritarian people who want all the creature comforts and immediate gratification of their desires. Anxiety, loneliness, and feelings of entrapment haunt them.

This is also a "fatherless" generation. The mature, more powerful members of society are not to be trusted, and their younger heirs seem to prefer their own failures over belief in those who have already failed. Caught like animals in a trap, these people lash out at themselves and others. Nouwen's summary is an appropriate description of many of the victims Archer encounters in his professional life. In Macdonald's books many crimes are uncovered precisely because the young people in them have questioned or are searching for their antecedents.

Aloofness, Nouwen seems to be saying, is the worst posture for a person who wants to help. Troubled people need smiles, touches, handshakes, and, above all, concern. No one can help without getting involved. The greatest myth of leadership, he claims, is that people can be led out of the desert by someone who has never been there. He sees the ministry as there to remind people that in order to become liberated they must first acknowledge their mortality and their incompleteness. Thus the priest cannot wholly set himself apart—his active compassion is crucial:

> Through compassion it is possible to recognize that the craving for love that men feel resides also in our own hearts, that the cruelty that the world knows all too well is rooted in our own impulses. Through compassion we also sense our hope for forgiveness in our friends' eyes and our hatred in their bitter mouths. When they kill, we know that we could have done it; when they give life, we know that we can do the

same. For a compassionate man nothing human is alien: no joy and no sorrow, no way of living and no way of dying.

This compassion is authority because it does not tolerate the pressure of the in-group, but breaks through the boundaries between languages and countries, rich and poor, educated and illiterate. This compassion pulls people away from the fearful clique into the large world where they can see that every human face is the face of a neighbor. Thus the authority of compassion is the possibility of man to forgive his brother, because forgiveness is only real for him who has discovered the weakness of his friends and the sins of his enemy in his own heart and is willing to call every human being his brother.2

It is striking how well Archer fits Nouwen's idea of the compassionate healer. Loner though he may be, Archer is *not* aloof. He is not only aware of the problems his clients are facing, he has been in trouble in the past himself.

Although Archer has consciously chosen law over the criminal life, he has suffered a major failure in his own relations that continues to haunt him. He is no cipher, nor is he simply a philosophical camera allowing Macdonald to project his own insights into the story. Archer is very much a part of his world; he understands people because he can empathize with them. He listens, evaluates, serves as a "confessor," and assigns penance, just as a priest would while serving a parishioner.

Archer has moved beyond Spade and Marlowe, the "gifted gumshoes," to become a very special kind of hero, the detective as healer.

III.

WHAT MAKES LEW TICK?

It was one of those paintings concerning which only the painter could tell when it was finished. I had never seen anything quite like it: a cloudy mass like a dark thought in which some areas of brighter color stood out like hope or fear. It must have been very good or very bad, because it gave me a frison.

—*The Zebra-Striped Hearse*

Although, as we have seen, the hard-boiled detective can be assigned a symbolic value as priest to a troubled world, Ross Macdonald has not made an abstraction out of Lew Archer. His description is clear-cut. He is physically large, enough so that people believe he has been an athlete, usually assuming that he once played football (as he had in high school). In *The Galton Case* he is six feet tall and weighs 190 pounds; in *The Doomsters* he is 6'2". Whatever his actual height, he dresses well and recognizes quality when he sees it.

He carries a briefcase like any other professional. He makes a good impression on his clients because he is articulate. He does not let himself get drunk and avoids driving when he is tired. He likes to eat, (mostly medium rare steaks and ham-and-eggs.) He drinks a great deal of coffee and, on special occasions, enjoys a Gibson. He is not ashamed to ask for beer at gatherings of the elite. A smoker in his early days, he has given it up. He is not a "hard" man in any sense, shedding tears, and occasionally becoming violently ill over the deaths of people he knows.

The Artful Dodger

Although Archer's educational background is seemingly that of an ordinary detective, he has had some college background. Archer has never completed a degree, yet he encompasses a strong feel for the arts that fits his humanist role very well.

Examining the following Archer titles, however, leads one to the conclusion that Archer *is* knowledgeable in things artistic. He has an eye for nature's beauty, and he is not hesitant at evaluating his

21

wealthy clients' taste. The specific comments below graphically demonstrate Lew Archer's expertise in the world of art and artists.

"THE BEARDED LADY." Lew visits the studio of Hugh Western, a friend from his service days, after seeing a notice of Western's show in the Los Angeles papers. As he enters the studio, he recognizes a typical working artist's environment and identifies various objects and mediums. He passes through the museum storeroom, reflecting that the painter of an old gilt-framed picture "deserved to be hung, if the picture didn't."[1] He recalls that Western had expressed the view, during their war experiences, that "the jungle was as safe as a scene by Le Douanier Rousseau."[2] He immediately recognizes Sarah Silliman as the nude model for a mutilated charcoal sketch. Finally locating an ostensibly stolen Chardin painting, he describes it with simple appreciation: "The boy in the blue waist-coat was there in the frame, watching the apple, which looked good enough to eat after more than two hundred years."[3]

THE MOVING TARGET. Archer admires "a painting of a clock, a map, and a woman's hat arranged on a dressing-table. Time, space, and sex. It looked like a Kuniyoshi."[4] The Hackett's gallery contains superb art, a Kokoschka, a Picasso, and the Klee Mrs. Hackett sold to her husband before their marriage. Their comfortable leather-and-steel chair is a Bauhaus. Archer sees "a man in a geometrical maze [which] seemed to show that the man and the maze were continuous with each other."[5] Stephen Hackett is a man, literally, in a maze, like the man in the Klee.

THE DROWNING POOL. Lew recognizes a Rivera reproduction hanging in a motel room.

THE WAY SOME PEOPLE DIE. A print of Van Gogh's ever-popular *Sunflowers* hangs in Keith Dalling's apartment, but the cheerfulness of the art cannot mask the owner's' unhappiness.

THE IVORY GRIN. Lew admires Mrs. Singleton's series of Chinese paintings depicting the stages of man's journey through life. He is aware that the man's ear-lugs represent wisdom. Among the other paintings he recognizes a Watteau or a Pragonard.

FIND A VICTIM. The office of District Attorney Westmore features a pair of Don Freeman lithographs. Lew spots Paul Klee reproductions in Cassie Hildreth's room, but feels embarrassed when forced to admit he had not noticed the Praxiteles *Hermes*.

BLACK MONEY. The Tappingers decorate with Van Goghs and Gauguins, their walls full of post-Impressionist reproductions representing a world of sunshine and brilliance ironically at odds with their troubled, drab existence.

THE GALTON CASE. Archer spends some time looking at what he calls "ancestor-worship" art:

> portraits of Spanish dons, ladies in hoop skirts with bare monolithic bosoms, a Civil War officer in blue, and several gentlemen in nineteenth-century suits with sour nineteenth-century pusses between their whiskers. The one I liked best depicted a group of top-hatted tycoons watching a bulldog-faced tycoon hammer a gold spike into a railroad tie. There was a buffalo in the background, looking sullen.[6]

THE WYCHERLY WOMAN. Catherine Wycherly's work, Archer observes, was "composed of blobs and splashes of raw color. It was one of those paintings which are either very advanced or very backward, I can never tell which."[7] Wycherly looks at the painting "as if it were a Rorshach test he had failed" and announces that he is going to have it taken down.

THE CHILL. A college student is described as a "tall Toulouse-Lautrec."

THE GOODBYE LOOK. Lew identifies the primitive perspective of an oil painting of early Pacific Point in the Chalmer's mansion.

THE UNDERGROUND MAN. Lew observes that the headlights of a station wagon were "swiping like long paint brushes at the tree trunks."[8] He knows Ellen Kilpatrick is not a good painter, observing: "The walls were hung with canvases. Most of them were unframed, and their whorls and splotches of color looked unfinished, perhaps unfinishable."[9]

✶✶✶✶✶✶✶✶✶✶✶✶✶✶✶

Two Lew Archer novels are set exclusively in the art world, and the detective's ability to move comfortably in that milieu is tied directly to his success in solving the cases.

THE ZEBRA-STRIPED HEARSE

Burke Damis is a talented artist involved with Harriet Blackwell. Her father disapproves of him and hires Archer to investigate his background. As Archer observes laconically, "I've known a few painters. The young unrecognized ones have a special feeling about accepting things from other people. They live off the county while they do their work. All most of them want is a north light and enough money to buy paints and eat."10 Although Archer suspects the young man's motives, he *is* fascinated with his paintings.

In his search Archer goes to Ajijic where he meets several artists and patrons connected with Damis. Chauncey Reynolds tries to engage Archer in a discussion of Sir Joshua Reynolds' artistic and critical skills, but the detective says, "I'm not too hep artistically,"11 (a patent untruth in view of some of his other observations.) Among the family portraits described is what Archer believes to be a Gilbert Stuart, identifiable to him by its weight and finish, and the 1812 uniform worn by the subject.

He visits Anne Castle and learns from her what is "representational" art. He obtains Damis' self-portrait, and interestingly, he observes that one of Damis' eyes in the portrait is larger than the other—a symbolic *private eye* perhaps?

Back in Los Angeles Archer takes the portrait to his friend, art expert Manny Meyer, who immediately identifies the artist as Bruce Campion, a man so talented that it doesn't really matter that he is wanted by the police for his wife's murder! Up to now Archer failed to connect Burke Damis with the Dolly Stone Campion case. Finding the artist, though, has led to the crime. Archer goes on to exonerate the artist of the murder, observing that, while artists may be hard to get along with, they rarely stab people to death with icepicks!

THE BLUE HAMMER

Although Bruce Campion is innocent, some artists *do* commit violent crimes. Hired simply to recover a stolen painting, Archer learns that the artist, Richard Chantry, had disappeared some thirty years earlier under mysterious circumstances. The disappearance of the painting and that of the painter seem somehow to be intertwined. Jack Biemeyer, Archer's client, says he prefers "a picture of the biggest hole in the ground I'd ever seen"12 to any real art. The "hole" is his Arizona copper mine (which also is linked to the past Archer uncovers in the course of the novel.)

The Biemeyer's daughter, Doris (whom Archer compares to "a Chirico figure in the receding distance of the house"13), has a friend, Fred Johnson, a university student, who is also a docent at the local art museum. He is a suspect in the theft because the painting had intrigued him as a possible Chantry "memory" picture—painted not directly from a living model, but from the artist's memory of her. Meanwhile Paul Grimes, the agent who sold the painting to the Biemeyers, has also inexplicably disappeared.

Archer discovers a copy of a letter written to Chantry's wife at the time of his disappearance. The letter is full of artists' prattle about needing new horizons, the shallowness of Arizona history, and his desire to be alone to explore his own mind, like Gauguin. Ruth Biemeyer thinks it is a beautiful letter, but Archer feels only pity for Chantry's deserted wife, Francine. When he visits her she argues against the idea that Chantry painted the Biemeyer acquisition. Paul Grimes, she protests, sold them an imitation of a style Chantry had abandoned. Her hostility makes Archer suspicious.

Archer re-examines Chantry's work in the museum's shrine with his detective's eyes:

> The first pictures I looked at resembled windows into
> an alternative world, like the windows that jungle
> travelers used to watch the animals at night. But the
> animals in Chantry's painting seemed to be on the
> verge of becoming human. Or perhaps they were hu-
> man beings devolving into animals. [14]

Francine describes her husband's paintings as "Creation pictures—the artist's imaginative conception of evolution."[15] All were painted in six months in a single creative outburst, she claims. But before Archer can unravel these confusing details, he needs to find out where Grimes had acquired the so-called Chantry painting. This in turn leads him to other artists and dealers. When he finds Grimes's abandoned car it is full of paintings which cannot possibly be Chantrys.

> They didn't look like much of anything. There were a
> few seascapes and beach scenes, which looked like
> minor accidents, and a small portrait of a woman,
> which looked like a major one. But I didn't entirely
> trust my eye or my judgment. [16]

He takes them to Arthur Planter, a well-known art critic, who identifies one of the works as a Jacob Whitmore seascape, an early, and clearly, a clumsy work. Planter judges Whitmore to be totally incapable of producing much of value, or even of forging works by a better artist.

Coincidentally, Whitmore has been discovered drowned in the ocean *the day before*. Though the seascape now seems more meaningful, Archer still can't make the connection. He visits Whitmore's studio where the artist's girlfriend informs him that Paul Grimes had purchased *all* of Whitmore's paintings in order to obtain the only one that was *not* a Whitmore. By this time Archer is suspicious enough to ask for an autopsy of Whitmore's body, which reveals that the painter had indeed drowned in fresh water, then was thrown into the ocean. Now there is a pattern—and a homicide.

Simon Lashman, an Arizonian painter familiar with Chantry's past, says of Chantry's model, Mildred Mead "the woman's half-emerging features looked like [a] face struggling up out of the limbo of

25

the past."17 From Lashman, Archer learns that Richard Chantry had had a brother, William Mead, also a painter, who had imitated Richard, the better artist of the two brothers, then compounded the wrong by attempting to steal his brother's superior paintings and pass them off as his own. He died a tragic death before he could put this villainous scheme into motion. Lashman comments that Chantry's subsequent disappearance was what made him famous.

The final solution to the crime occurs when Archer suddenly realizes that the painting represents Mildred Mead as the Virgin Mary and Richard Chantry (an assumed self-portrait) as Christ. William, the man whom everyone assumed was already dead, was explaining that the brothers had switched places. Richard *is* dead, and William replaced him. Richard had been brutally beaten to death by his brother and identified incorrectly as William, by their mother. A conspiracy had long covered the whole episode. William Mead has spent the rest of his life like a caged animal, pacified by alcohol and art supplies in an ugly, rundown, locked house—the equivalent of the alternative world so evident in his work. Paul Grimes, who discovered the ugly secret, has also been beaten to death, probably at the hands of the maniacal William.

As he concludes the case, Archer tells Francine that William Mead is still a talented artist in spite of his mental and physical deterioration. He is astonished that the drunken old man was responsible for the world of his paintings; but then, he muses, "his essential life might have gone into that world and left him empty."18 William Mead actually lived in that alternative world Archer saw the first time he looked at the "Richard Chantry" creation pictures.

Thus Francine is not far from wrong when she snaps, "Apparently you're an art critic as well as a detective."19 No one has ever paid more attention to Chantry's work than Lew Archer, private detective, whose interest in art has helped him solve a murder dating back thirty years in the past.

It is clear that Archer is much more familiar with artists, works, techniques, and styles of art than the average P.I.

L. A. Law

Archer's knowledge of art comes, to a certain degree, from his acquaintance with artists coupled with his constant curiosity. He listens to and remembers all that people tell him.

His legal knowledge comes from the same sources—acquaintances like Bert Graves, Gordon Sable, Jerry Marks, and particularly Peter Colton, for whom he has worked. He knows, respects, and upholds the law of his society.

Macdonald often alludes to Archer's awareness of the law.

THE WAY SOME PEOPLE DIE. An incident where Archer takes a heavy screwdriver and easily picks the Yale-type spring lock is rare. It is important to note that Archer almost always operates *within* the law, unlike many other hard-boiled detectives. He is familiar enough with the results of criminal behavior not to emulate it. Archer, most often, comes down squarely on the side of law and order.

THE IVORY GRIN. Archer picks up Heiss's telegram but does not open it until he knows the other detective is dead, since it is a crime to open someone else's mail while he is still alive.

THE ZEBRA-STRIPED HEARSE. Lew asks Nelson Karp to return his tip as soon as he realizes that the desk clerk will be a witness in a murder trial and should not have to admit that he took any money. He will be paid as a witness, Archer tells him (but doesn't say how much.)

THE CHILL. In a conference with lawyer Jerry Marks, Archer tells him that he doubts Dolly Kincaid is legally insane according to the "McNaughton rule."

THE FAR SIDE OF THE DOLLAR. Stella is talked into returning to her parents when Lew informs her that her refusal makes him responsible for contributing to the delinquency of a minor. (He also confirms that there is a law allowing men to be arrested for adultery, although it is not often enforced.)

BLACK MONEY. He warns Harry Hendricks that bribery and impersonating an officer can lead to felony charges.

SLEEPING BEAUTY. Archer warns Dr. Brokaw that he is obligated to report his treatment of a gunshot wound to the police.

THE BLUE HAMMER. Archer's knowledge of the law is all practical experience, however, and not from any law school, as the District Attorney is quick to point out.

Soothing The Savage Beast

I watched her white hands picking their way through the artificial boogie-woogie jungle. The music followed them like giant footsteps rustling in metallic undergrowth. You could see the shadow of the giant and hear his trip-hammer heartbeat. She was hot.
—*The Moving Target*

As these few passages illustrate, Archer exhibits an unusual sensitivity to musicians and the music they make.

"FIND THE WOMAN." He shows off his knowledge of classical music by referring to the choreography of *Danse Macabre*.

"GONE GIRL." In this story Archer recognizes the *Dead March* from *Saul*.

THE MOVING TARGET. Archer goes to the "Wild Piano" to hear Betty Fraley play, and to question her about his case. Her playing is "threading the laughter in a melancholy counterpoint"[20] and her movements reflected in the keyboard mirror are described as having "a hurried fatality." Betty, like trombonist Sam Jackman, has been involved with drugs, but unlike Sam, she is still addicted. Later her records will provide Archer with a clue to solving his case. Archer is a connoisseur of jazz music, which allows him to break the ice with Jackman, in spite of their mutual suspicions.

THE DROWNING POOL. Lew considers the Furious Five's performance to be maltreatment of instruments!

> The guitar bit chunks from the chromatic scale and spat them out in rapid fire without chewing them. The drummer hit everything he had, drums, taps, cymbals, stamped on the floor, beat the rungs of his chair, banged the chrome rod that supported the microphone.[21]

THE CHILL. Archer recognizes a tenor and soprano duet from *La Bohème*.

THE FAR SIDE OF THE DOLLAR. Lew teases Stella by quoting Gilbert and Sullivan's "Never? Hardly ever..."[22]

BLACK MONEY. Peter is described as going through the motions just as "the merry villagers would troop in for the nuptial dance,"[23] indicating Archer's familiarity with the conventions of light opera.

Lew of All Trades

There are other areas of Archer's expertise we might mention. He is familiar enough with literature to be comfortable with Chad Bolling, the poet in *The Galton Case*, and at ease enough with academic matters to fit in with people like Dean Roy Bradshaw in *The Chill* and Professor Allan Bosch in *Black Money*. Although he denies it, he knows enough about drama, poetry, and modern literature to evaluate and understand it, and he has been known to make references to such works as Tolstoi's *Resurrection, Waiting for Godot*, "The Vision of Mirza," and *Hamlet*. He freely admits that he has read both *The Psychopathology of Everyday Life* and Gandhi's *Truth*.[24] And anyone who has the nerve to say "The quality of the shirred eggs Bercy was not strained,"25 or "Look to your lady, Mr. Wycherly,"26 can hardly be considered an unread clod! Archer has shown his knowledge and appreciation of a myriad of topics, including fine furniture, architecture (he describes Dr. Sponti's fingers making first a Norman arch and then a Gothic one as he skirts the issues they are discussing), sports, contemporary issues, food, history, myth, academic institutions, psychology, clothing, the movie industry, ballet, boats, Latin, Spanish, and—of course—the ways of criminals. He is truly a Renaissance man.

But how did he acquire all this knowledge? The temptation is to assume that, when he is not working on a case, Archer is at his desk, feet up, reading some classic or other. But the books do not provide support for that thesis.

In *The Far Side of the Dollar* Lew sits at Susanna Drew's patio table while she explains the identity myths her father taught her. This is obviously one way in which the detective learns. He is clearly an excellent listener and has almost total recall of what he has heard.

In *The Chill* Archer enters a drug store and scans the paperbacks while he waits for Mrs. Hoffman and Mrs. Delony. He buys a book on ancient Greek philosophy and reads the chapter on Zeno. His curiosity had been picqued earlier when two students talked about Achilles and the tortoise, Zeno's paradox of time.

The bits and pieces of knowledge he thus accumulates are not typical of those which appeal to the average detective. His interests seem much more ecclectic and represent not only a curiosity about his world, but about the many types of people he encounters in it. This variety of interests undoubtedly aids in his ministry to the society in which he lives.

IV.

THE CALLING

When I went into police work in 1935, I believed that evil was a quality some people were born with, like a harelip. A cop's job was to find those people and put them away. But evil isn't so simple. Everybody has it in him, and whether it comes out in his actions depends on a number of things. Environment, opportunity, economic pressure, a piece of bad luck, a wrong friend. The trouble is a cop has to go on judging people by rule of thumb, and acting on the judgment.

—*The Moving Target*

After an unpleasant episode in *The Blue Hammer* Archer tells Mrs. Johnson: "I chose this job, or it chose me. There's a lot of human pain involved in it, but I'm not looking for another job."[1]

The priesthood is an occupation so special that the term "calling" is often applied to it, and those who enter it have the conviction that their work has chosen them rather than the other way around. Although there is the obvious commitment to a special service—experience, good business skills, knowledge of human relations, and certain tools of the trade are also necessary to success. A priest (or a detective for that matter) must not only have the feeling that he has been called, he needs to be good at what he does in order to serve his flock effectively.

The Uses of the Past

I sat in my brand-new office with the odor of paint in my nostrils and waited for something to happen. I had been back on the Boulevard for one day. This was the beginning of the second day. Below the window, flashing in the morning sun, the traffic raced and roared with a noise like battle. It made me nervous. It made me want to move. I was all dressed up in civilian clothes with no place to go and nobody to go with.

—"Find the Woman"

31

Lew Archer is eminently qualified to be a detective. In *The Name is Archer*, Ross Macdonald hints at the past that has led to Archer's calling. In his very first case, the new detective sits alone, waiting for a client, and wearing the new suit he has purchased with $150 of his army separation money. Although he has only been out of the army for one week, Archer already has the reputation of a man who has "never been bought." He does, however, trust the police, one of the traits that distinguishes him from most of the other hard-boiled detectives. In fact, in this introductory story he identifies *with* the police, even saying, "I sort of am the police."2

The first specific mention of his police experience comes in "Gone Girl" when he answers the recurring question, "You a police-man?" with "I have been."3 In "The Bearded Lady" he bridles at an insult by snapping, "I'm not exactly an amateur. I used to be a cop."4 As a matter of fact, Archer exudes "ex-copness." Often, through people's automatic assumption that he represents the police, he is able to bluff his way into the information he seeks. Most of the time, however, he admits his police experience grudgingly.

Throughout the course of the novels such information creeps into the narrative insidiously. He first puts forth his philosophy of detection in the *The Moving Target*. Speeding along in his search for Leo Sampson, Archer admits to Miranda that he loves "tame danger"—being able to take his life in his hands without the actual risk of losing it. He tells her that he inherited his job from another man, a younger and more idealistic Archer, who once believed that the world was composed of good and bad people and that when you identified the ones who were evil, you could place blame on them and punish them.

His consistent psychoanalysis of people and his even more consistent refusal to accept pat answers from any of them seem traceable to this early statement. He senses Mrs. Dreen's dislike for her missing daughter and thus begins to distrust her every action, even when she merely crosses her legs. His inability to function as a policeman probably came about when this quest for justice was blocked by official versions of reality. His past experience is so basic in helping Archer understand himself, the police, and the people involved in crime that it is mentioned constantly throughout the novels.

It is also significant, particularly in the light of his revelation to Miranda, that so many of his cases lead to others that were never solved because the police, unable to come to any conclusion, simply created an official report and closed the investigation.

When Archer states to Mrs. Sampson in *The Moving Target*, "I'm the new-type detective,"5 he's doing more than referring to the fact that he doesn't drink before lunch like Spade and Marlowe. He really is of a new breed, one who *cares* about his clients and the people whose lives he touches.

More specific details come from *The Moving Target* when Albert Graves inquires, "Why did you quit the Long Beach force, Lew?" "I couldn't stand podex osculation [ass-kissing]. And I didn't like dirty politics. Anyway, I didn't quit, I was fired."[6] When he first sees Ralph Knudson at a party in *The Drowning Pool*, Archer tells Maude Slocum that after five years on the Long Beach force he recognizes the pattern from which policemen are cut. Shrewdly analyzing Archer's passion for justice and truth, Maude tells him that he has the intelligence and personality for a better, more prestigious job. When he retorts that he does not want to be like Knudson, Archer's bitterness surfaces. "I worked in a municipal police department for five years, and then I quit. There were too many cases where the official version clashed with the facts I knew."[7] The conflict between a policeman's public and private conscience was something that Archer was unable to handle. He is above all else a highly ethical man.

Throughout the novels he is described as acting, looking, and even smelling like a cop, a fact he acknowledges in *The Way Some People Die*. "I was police-trained and the harness left its marks on me."[8] Lieutenant Gary at first is disappointed in Archer when he thinks he is working with Dowser. He chides Archer for his lack of cooperation, but then tells him that since he has never tried to cheat the police and because Peter Colton speaks highly of him, they won't arrest him.

Archer's confrontations with the law have some of the smart-mouthed quality of Marlowe's altercations, particularly when he counters Gary's accusation, by suggesting that a criminal like Dowser must have had police protection. Gary returns, "Don't tell me about Dowser's payoff. I know. I also know why you left the Long Beach force. You wouldn't take Sam Schneider's monthly cut, and he forced you out."[9] Thus we learn that Archer was indeed an honest policeman who could not function within a tarnished system.

On the whole, however, the police with whom Archer deals are usually depicted as fair, and even admirable. In fact, Archer must have done a decent job, since by the time we reach *The Ivory Grin* he reports that he was a detective-sergeant.

In *Find A Victim* a new aspect of Archer's past experience with the police is suggested. Archer was once tempted to become a criminal himself, and as a result, he is better equipped to recognize the fine line between good and bad behavior. While interrogating 21-year-old Leonard Bozey, a small-time crook, Lew recalls:

> I had lifted cars myself when I was a kid, shared joy-rides and brawls with the lost gangs in the endless stucco maze of Los Angeles. My life had been like Bozey's up to a point. Then a whiskey-smelling plain-clothes man caught me stealing a battery from

the back room of a Sears Roebuck store in Long
Beach. He stood me against the wall and told me
what it meant and where it led. He didn't turn me in.
I hated him for years, and never stole again....
Bozey....But for the grace of an alcoholic detective
sergeant, me.[10]

Another factor in Archer's choice of profession is revealed in
The Barbarous Coast when Archer's memory of Raymond Campbell, a
silent movie star, surfaces:

I could remember a time in the early twenties when
Campbell's serials filled the Long Beach movie house
on Saturday afternoons. Me they had filled with in-
spiration: his Inspector Fate of Limehouse series had
helped to make me a cop, for good or ill. And when
the cops went sour, the memory of Inspector Fate had
helped me out of the Long Beach force.[11]

The romantic dream world of films won out over the unpleasant realities of Long Beach street life and a demoralizing brush with
political corruption.

In *The Doomsters* Archer must come to grips with his personal
guilt, and he establishes himself as a detective who has been *part* of the
fallen world himself. This story reveals much more about Archer personally than the other books. In it he empathizes with the murderess,
once he establishes her guilt, and assures her that he does not hate her.
The fact that he has been involved in a tragic (and unnecessary) set of
murders deepens his awareness that crime and punishment are not simply matters of law enforcement.

I was an ex-cop, and the words came hard. I had to
say them, though, if I didn't want to be stuck for the
rest of my life with the old black-and-white picture,
the idea that there were just good people and bad people, and everything would be hunky-dory if the good
people locked up the bad ones or wiped them out with
small personalized nuclear weapons.[12]

In *The Doomsters*, ill-fated Tom Rica and Lew's ex-wife Sue
are constant reminders to Archer that he has not totally come up to his
own standards. He knows he has let Tom down when he could just as
easily have had the same effect on the boy that the old cop had had on
him.

I'd been a street boy in my time, gang-fighter, thief, pool-room lawyer. It was a fact that I didn't like to remember. It didn't fit in with the slick polaroid picture I had of myself of the rising young man of mystery who frequented beach clubs in the company of starlets. Who groped for a fallen brightness in private white sand, private white bodies, expensive peroxide hair.[13]

Tom Rica had information that could have saved the lives lost in this novel, but Archer brushed him off. Years later the detective remembers how Tom affected him. "I saw myself when I was a frightened junior-grade hood in Long Beach, kicking the world in the shins because it wouldn't dance for me."[14]

Much of Archer's respect for the law, then, is based on the fact that he himself ran afoul of it as a teenager. When he learns more about Davy Spanner, who is regarded as a vicious, psychotic kidnapper in *The Instant Enemy*, Archer tells Davy's probation officer, "I was one of the ones who turned out different and better. Slightly better, anyway. I joined the cops instead of the hoods."[15]

By the time *Sleeping Beauty* is published, Archer can remark quite casually that, "Most private detectives came out of police work. I used to be on the Long Beach force myself."[16] Still, in the final novel, *The Blue Hammer*, he seems uncomfortable with his past, thinking to himself when Mrs. Johnson asks if he is a policeman: "I had been when I was younger, and apparently it still showed to a cop-sensitive eye."[17]

Obviously, those five years on the police force, and the boyhood dream of righting wrongs that had its birth in the Long Beach movie house left an impact. The only other remotely job-related experiences he mentions are his Golden Glove boxing years, and one summer working on a dude ranch when he was seventeen.

The third leg of the triad which has influenced Archer's choice of profession comes almost certainly from his military service. If police experience is his first major qualification for his new line of work, the second is his stint as a soldier.

In "The Bearded Lady" Archer pays a visit to his old army buddy, Western, with whom he had been stationed in the Philippines. Silliman, one of the story's characters, easily puts Archer in his place: "He was only a retired admiral, and I'd been out of uniform for years, but he gave me a qualm."[18] These and other brief hints are the only background given in the first seven stories. The novels, as we have seen, divulge the rest of his past in greater detail.

The Moving Target involves a friend with whom he served previously, Albert Graves, an ex-District Attorney who recommends him to Mrs. Sampson. They remind each other of their service roles: Graves was in military government and Archer in intelligence, under

Peter Colton, who still supports him in his run-ins with authority. *The Drowning Pool* adds that he was an officer,[19] and in *The Way Some People Die* Archer reminisces about a brigadier he knew in Colon during the war:

> His hobby was hunting sharks in the open sea, with no equipment but a mask and a knife. I used to run his speedboat for him sometimes. Nobody on his staff could figure out why he did it. I asked him about it one day when he nearly got himself killed and I had to go in after him. He said that it gave him background for dealing with human beings. He was a very shy man for a general.[20]

Archer's service memories are not all pleasant. In *Find A Victim* he is down on his knees and elbows, ready for a shoot-out. "The position brought back the smells of cordite and flame-throwers and scorched flesh, the green and bloody springtime of Okinawa."[21] The same kind of image appears in *The Wycherly Woman* when he tries to imagine the islands where he had been in battle as vacation spots: "The South Pacific I remembered smelled of cordite and flame throwers."[22]

Colonel Blackwell in *The Zebra-Striped Hearse* was an undistinguished regular army officer, and Ralph Hillman in *The Far Side of the Dollar* was a navy captain. Both have problems with children who run away, and both make difficult situations worse. Archer knows the type, however, and can handle them.

In *Sleeping Beauty* his wartime memories are, perhaps, deliberately vague, and he places no special emphasis on his being at Okinawa, the scene of the critical fire on the *Canaan Sound* on May 22, 1945 which destroyed Captain Somerville's ship and ruined his career. The murder of Allie Russo, however, has destroyed several lives, and Archer's past helps him understand the incident:

> I neither believed the Captain nor disbelieved him. I had been in the Army, though, and traveled on naval vessels. I knew something about the power of their captains to create their own reality aboard ship—a power that sometimes could extend long past the event, and shape the record of official inquiries.[23]

The Root of All Evil

Six hundred dollars was what I got working for a full week, and I didn't work every week. I had about three hundred dollars in the bank, about two hundred in cash. I owned an equity in the car and some

> *clothes and furniture. My total net worth, after nearly twenty years in the detective business was in the neighborhood of thirty-five hundred dollars....On the other hand, I answered my self-pity, I was doing what I wanted to be doing.*
>
> *—The Far Side of the Dollar*

Archer's experiences as an ex-juvenile delinquent, an ex-cop, and an ex-serviceman have qualified him superbly for the profession he now takes so seriously as a business. He runs a one-man agency, as he states in "The Suicide," but co-opts other private agents like Arnie and Phyllis and Willie Mackey. He calls on lawyers, the FBI, police, coroners, journalists, and many other colleagues to assist him while conducting his investigations.

Archer works for money, though not much of it, in today's terms. He accepts $100 for his work in "Wild Goose Chase." His fee in "The Suicide" is stated as $50 a day. He feels flush when he collects $1,000 for work done in San Francisco. He asks for $75 a day in *The Moving Target*, but fails to get the money up front, and Bert Graves only gives him $60. By the time of *Black Money*, Archer has learned to collect his money in advance because he knows once the case is over, clients can be reluctant to pay up.

Archer *is* concerned with keeping his business profitable. He tells Peter Jamieson that the $100 fee isn't really a great deal: "Actually, it's just enough to get by on. I don't work all the time, and I have to maintain an office."[24] In *The Far Side of the Money* Archer, who owes Arnie Walters $600 for his work grouses that "Ralph Hillman, with his money, was letting me finance my own search for his son." Finally, Hillman relents and gives him $2,000. "I was back in business," Archer exults.[25]

He refers to his almost-paid-for car in *The Goodbye Look*, and *The Instant Enemy* finds him asking for "two days' pay and expenses, say two hundred and fifty"[26] which he gets. He notes, however, that the Sebastians have less than $200 in their bank account after paying him, and characteristically, he gives them their money's worth, not even taking time out to eat lunch.

By the time of *Sleeping Beauty*, Archer is charging $100 a day plus expenses, owes $300 in bills, and has $200 in his checking account, earmarked for rent. But he is content because he is in the middle of a case and his clients have money.[27] He does not flourish, but he survives.

Archer usually earns enough to maintain his honor and his integrity. In *The Ivory Grin* resenting the way that Una tosses a crumpled $100 bill at him "as if it were an old piece of Kleenex and I were a waste-basket,"[28] he pulls it out and offers it back to her. She mollifies him and he puts it back—only to toss it at her in real anger when he realizes she is using him. This time she keeps it, leaving him with a lonely wallet:

> I had no client, no good leads, not much money. Regret for Una's hundred-dollar bill was gnawing at me already, like a small hungry stomach ulcer.[29]

Throughout his career Archer is forced to turn down bribes and offers of less-than-honest employment. He keeps Clare's $26,390 in "The Suicide," but protects himself by giving her a receipt for it. The actor Terry Neville offers him a tainted "sheaf of bills," and he is forced to turn down $700 in "Gone Girl." Archer knocks out Hendryx's muscle-bound bodyguard in "The Bearded Lady," whereupon the questionable man announces: "I could find a use for you—a place in my organization."[30] Archer accepts a $100 bill in "Guilt-Edged Blonde," but he puts it all by itself in a separate pocket. Harlan offers him $1,000 in travelers checks to bury his sister and forget the incident, but Lew refuses to fulfill either request.

In *The Moving Target*, Troy offers him $700 of the night's gate from smuggling illegal aliens. Never one to be much disturbed by a gun at his head, Archer corrects Troy's figures: "One third of a hundred thousand is thirty-three thousand three hundred and thirty-three dollars and thirty-three cents."[31] Archer goes on to say that he wouldn't take his money anyway.

Though Stephen Hackett offers him $20 for his time at their first meeting, in *The Moving Target*, Mrs. Marburg, Hackett's wealthy mother, offers him $100,000 to get Stephen home safely after he is kidnapped. Learning just how evil the Hacketts are, he takes the check out of his office safe, shreds it, and tosses it out of his window in a shower of yellow confetti.

In *The Drowning Pool* Walter Kilbourne tells Archer to keep the $1,000 he finds and mind his own business. Kilbourne offers a receipt for services rendered which would make Archer an accessory. "I caught the implication." Archer muses. "I watched it grow in my mind into a picture of myself five years, ten years later, doing dirty errands for Walter Kilbourne and not being able to say no."[32] When Archer turns down the offer, Kilbourne doubles it. Again Archer says no and ends up in Dr. Melliotes' torture chamber for his trouble.

He goes ahead and gives Gretchen Keck the $10,000 he recovered from Reavis, knowing that she will just waste it.

> The money wouldn't do her any permanent good. She'd buy a mink coat or a fast car, and find a man to steal one or wreck the other. Another Reavis, probably. Still, it would give her something to remember different from the memories that she had. She had no

souvenirs and I had too many. I wanted no momentos of Reavis or Kilbourne.[33]

Archer does take Dowser's $100 bill in *The Way Some People Die* (having learned the hard way that gangsters don't like having people turn down their bribes) observing, "This money twisted in my hand like a fat green tomato-worm."[34] Later he turns over $100,000 worth of heroin to District Attorney Colton and uses it as a lever to get Dowser arrested.

In *The Instant Enemy* he gets two offers of money for *not* doing his job. Laurel Smith offers him $500 to stop looking for Davy, then doubles it and includes herself in the bargain.

In *The Barbarous Coast* Frost offers Archer a job in his organization and an all-expense paid trip to Italy. "I wouldn't let you pay my way to Pismo Beach," he replies.[35] For his honesty he gets hospitalized by the resultant beating, although he has admitted that:

> I want it very badly....But I can't take this money. It wouldn't belong to me, I would belong to it. It would expect me to do things, and I would have to do them. Sit on the lid of this mess of yours, the way Marfeld did, until dry rot set in.[36]

In the last two novels Archer also refuses to cover up the truth. In *Sleeping Beauty*, Jack Lennox asks if Archer would keep quiet about the whole affair for $100,000, and Mrs. Chantry offers him an unspecified amount to do the same in *The Blue Hammer*. Archer tells Mrs. Chantry that he prefers to be bribed with information. Obviously, money is not the main reason for Archer's professional dedication.

Most of Archer's work is not glamorous. His career has involved: divorce cases, body-guard duty, surveillance, commitment trials, involvement with narcotics distribution studies, testifying in numerous court cases, and checking on false registrations for a hotel association. He has allowed some people whom he was hired to find escape, and he has had a client's wife die from an overdose of sleeping pills. He has learned a great deal about mental illness and the ways of gangsters from his work.

Peter Colton calls him "a run-down divorce detective" in *The Moving Target*,[37] and in *The Drowning Pool* he tells a motel owner euphemistically, "I've done a good deal of work in and about Hollywood." What he really means is that he has been "peeping on fleabag hotel rooms, untying marital knots, blackmailing blackmailers out of business. Dirty, heavy, hot work on occasion."[38] In "Gone Girl" he calls himself "a garbage collector in the moral field,"[39] and in *The Barbarous Coast* he tells George Wall that he's "the indigent's Florence Nightingale."[40]

His everyday work is often dull. In *The Ivory Grin* he says
"My job was a walking job and a driving job, but mainly a sitting and
waiting job."[41] In what may be a key statement made in *The Moving
Target*, Archer admits that "The graduates of the police schools make a
big thing of scientific detection, and that has its place. But most of my
time is spent watching people and judging them."[42]

Archer likes to be free to follow facts wherever they lead. He
does not, however, accept things at face value, which is why he is so
successful in digging up hidden motives, and even, on occasion, buried
bodies. "Policemen and prosecutors are usually glad to accept the facts,
or the pseudo-facts that fit their case,"[43] he says in *The Chill*.

In *The Doomsters* he identifies with psychiatric caseworker
Rose Parish because he and she operate on the same wavelength; their
time is spent talking to ordinary people and hoping for truth to surface.
Archer's stance toward a witness is neither belief nor disbelief. He
never argues with a witness, only listens, then acts on what he hears.

He has a compelling drive to find the complete truth with or
without payment or client. Sometimes, even after the missing person is
found, the case is not over. In "The Suicide" he declares: "I was
tempted to go away and send her the money and forget the whole thing.
But the need to finish it pushed me, imperative as a gun at my back."[44]
This same compelling need gets him into trouble when he encounters a
tough woman ex-cop in "Guilt-Edged Blonde" who advises him to im-
prove his tailing technique.

Archer does not mind being given advice, but he is sensitive to
slurs cast on his professional ability. When a Hollywood writer describes Archer's work as unearthing "people's guilty secrets and
[exposing] them to the eyes of a scandalized world,"[45] Lew is tempted
to start a fight. Neither does he appreciate Dr. Frey's observation, "So
you are an altruist, are you? A Hollywood culture-hero in a sports
coat? You propose to clean the Augean stables single-handed?"[46]

When Mildred Fleming wonders why he works so hard on the
case—Is it for money?—he replies:

> Maude gave me two hundred dollars: that's all gone
> by now. But once I'm in a case I sort of like to stay
> through to the end. It's more than curiosity. She
> must have died for a reason. I owe it to her or myself
> to find out the reason, to see the whole thing clear.[47]

Sheriff Church accuses Archer of breaking and entering, and
warns him off the case. An angry Archer counters that his break-ins are
neater than that, then he turns the tables on Church, accusing him of
conspiring with hoods and of taking the public's money while ob-
structing the solution of a homicide. Lew resents being accused of
sloppy work and has no patience with those who do their jobs poorly.

V.

SLEEPING WITH THE ENEMY

*I tried to move like a neutral in the no man's land be-
tween the lawless and the law. But when the shooting
started I generally knew which side I belonged on.*
                                    —*Sleeping Beauty*

When Kate Kerrigan accuses Archer of having a "crimeside
manner"—of being "nice" to her during a psychological third-degree,
he is stung. "I don't deny I've been tempted to use people, play on
their feelings, push them around. Those are the occupational diseases
of my job....This is a dirty business I'm in. All I can do is watch myself and keep it as clean as I can."[1] He is equally hurt by Dr. Brokaw's
accusation in *Sleeping Beauty* that his real goal is to maintain a punitive
society's smooth operation by keeping the arrest rate up:

> Polarized by Brokaw, as perhaps Brokaw was polar-
> ized by me, I felt very little different from the man in
> harness I had been twenty years before when I re-
> signed from the Long Beach police force.[2]

He is still "fuzz."
    Archer continually analyzes his own motives and, although he
is primarily driven by his need to know the truth, he is also compassionate, and he needs the approval of society.
    "Social mobility is my stock in trade," Archer announces in
"The Bearded Lady." He gets along with every type of person, Sometimes he plays dumb: "I'll give you my autograph, only I sign it with
an 'X,'" he quips to Alan Taggert, who says that being a detective is
most kids' dream. "Most kids don't get stuck with the dream," Archer
replies. Miranda snaps, "Don't you ever get bored with yourself playing the dumb detective?"[3]
    In *The Barbarous Coast* Tobias, a college student, is disap-
pointed with Archer's profession because it isn't idea-oriented. He admits, "It's a rough life....you see people at their worst."[4] Dolly Lang
reacts differently in *The Wycherly Woman*. When Archer tells her he is

"a kind of poorman's sociologist,"[5] she incorporates his ideas into the paper she is writing on the causes of juvenile delinquency .

Archer mixes with lower classes, gangsters, and experienced crooks in the early works, but gradually begins to function as an upper-middle class detective as he progresses. He is comfortable with Hollywood types, movie actresses, agents, writers, with the police, with artists, college professors, students, and young people of all kinds.

He does not always approve of his clients or of the people with whom he must deal in his cases. Jack Biemeyer grumbles, "I know how you private dicks operate. You let the men in uniform do the work and then you step in and take the credit,"[6] and Archer wants to hang up on him. He fails to listen to Tom Rica and Bess Tappinger because of their outward appearances, and lives to regret it. But to his amusement, FBI man Thorndike (in *The Instant Enemy*) "was a little superior, like a teacher giving an oral quiz to a not very apt pupil. I didn't mind. I had brought Hackett in. He hadn't."[7]

Though he claims just the opposite, he often becomes emotionally involved with his clients. He tells Maude Slocum that he must "use" her family as a base from which to operate. When she argues that he is just an employee, he corrects her by stating he is an independent contractor. And he has been known to walk out on a client (although normally he works especially hard to establish a close relationship with the people he works for). In *The Goodbye Look* he resents Mrs. Chalmers' manipulative ways because "She had wrecked my rapport with her, and any possible rapport with her husband."[8] Often Archer's most difficult clients will become implicated in the crime.

He has no more use for a "bad" detective than he would have for a "bad" cop. Maxfield Heiss, a Los Angeles investigator, lacks the necessary skills, tact, and honesty to be a good detective, thus hampering Lew's search for Lucy Champion. Heiss is a grotesque parody of the usually competent literary P.I., and he uses people without discrimination, showing no sympathy or respect for the human animal he hunts. He has already lost his licence for tampering with prospective jurors in a murder trial, and Archer wisely wants no part of him. A foolish, nervous man, Heiss continues the search even after he is fired. Archer suspects he sees an opportunity for blackmail. Heiss, by contrast, makes Archer look even better than usual.

In *The Far Side of the Dollar* Otto Sipe appears as the worst possible kind of inebriated hotel detective turned night watchman. "He was the kind of detective who gives our trade a bad name."[9] He had blackmailed Mrs. Hillman through pictures taken of her husband and Susanna Drew, and he is involved in Tommy Hillman's disappearance and Harley's corruption.

When Sidney Harrow, another amateur detective, is killed in *The Goodbye Look*, Archer feels he, too, has been tainted. "My brief dip into Sidney Harrow's life had left a stain on my nerves. Perhaps it reminded me too strongly of my own life. Depression threatened me like a sour smoke drifting in behind my eyes."[10]

In *The Instant Enemy* Jack Fleischer is working on the same case as Archer, but for a different reason. Their paths cross in unpleasant ways as they search for Davy Spanner. After a lawman has been shot, Archer visits the widow, who calls him "Jack" Archer. Once again he has been identified with the "wrong" side of the business—the man without ethics who causes more trouble than he cures.

Archer's innate compassion, however, can be extended even to these pariahs. In *Black Money* Harry Hendricks, an amateur detective, is put in jeopardy because of his ineptness. At first Archer feels scorn for him with his miniature camera, lack of licence, and paucity of tact and skill. But Archer relents when he finds Harry locked in the trunk of his wrecked Cadillac; Lew takes Harry to a private hospital and pays his bills rather than have him taken to the county hospital where he will not receive individualized treatment.

Archer's own ethics can sometimes be compromised, as when he gets Fay Estabrook drunk to pump information out of her. He feels guilty, but he does exactly the same thing to Johnson in *The Blue Hammer*. Although such actions propel his cases forward, Archer does not generally believe that the ends justify the means. "I try to be honest with honest people," he says in *The Galton Case*.[11]

In *The Goodbye Look* he tells Moira Smitheram that "The life is its own reward. I like to move into people's lives and then move out again. Living with one set of people in one place used to bore me."[12] He hesitates to question her too closely, because it would be using her, and when she decides to leave her husband, she makes it clear to him that he played no role in her decision. She is angry with herself for having made money from other people's suffering, and Archer can understand her feelings since he makes his living in much the same way.

> I try not to....When your income passes a certain
> point you lose touch. All of a sudden the other people
> look like geeks or gooks, expendables.[13]

His relationship with Moira is typical. He is able to learn much about people without ever losing his compassion for them.

Archer operates as an intermediary in many of his cases. Sometimes he negotiates a truce between the law and the accused criminal. Often, particularly in the later books, he becomes an agent for intervention in dysfunctional families because he hates to see people suffer. Mrs. Brighton in *The Blue Hammer* notes that it is strange for someone in his profession to care that much about the lives with which he is dealing. "But every now and then I have a chance to prevent a killing," he tells her. But he thinks to himself, "And every now and then I precipitated one."[14]

Brian Kilpatrick in *The Underground Man* tells Lew that he "smells like trouble."

> That stopped me for a minute. He had a salesman's insight into human weakness, and he'd touched on a fact which I didn't always admit to myself—that I sometimes served as a catalyst for trouble, not unwillingly.[15]

VI.

TOOLS OF THE TRADE

*Once I killed another man with my hands. I did it to
save my own life, but his blood is on my hands.*
  —*The Drowning Pool*

Although he is a philosopher, Archer is also practical. He begins his career wearing and using a gun. In *The Name is Archer* collection he is a party to violence just like any other hard-boiled detective.
He kills the gunman Gino in "Gone Girl." He shoots a man from Las
Vegas in "The Suicide"—then regrets it because the woman he is defending is not innocent. (The man, Jack Fidelity, however, turns out to
be suspected of shooting the gangster Bugsy Siegel!) In "Guilt-Edged
Blonde" he shoots Mrs. Nemo in the right arm as she skillfully reaches
for her .32 caliber revolver. In "The Sinister Habit" Archer kills Dol-
phine, a murderer, as he in turn is shooting Harlan. Up to this point in
Archer's career he is typically hard-boiled and capable of killing and
seeing people killed without distress.
  In *The Moving Target* Archer faces Puddler, a sadistic goon
who cowers in front of strong women—"a savage accidentally dropped
in the steel-and-concrete jungle, a trained beast of burden, a fighting
machine."[1] Although he is tied up and about to be killed, Archer taunts
Puddler into a fight. Lew, an expert swimmer, pulls his opponent under water and drowns him. Immediately he regrets the killing.
Strangely enough, the subsequent novels imply that Puddler was
Archer's *only* victim; thereafter he is commonly used as a symbol for
Archer's compassion for the person who murders out of desperation.
  In *The Drowning Pool* another man holding a gun on Archer
announces that he has never yet killed a man. He responds. "I
have....He kicked me in the head when I was down."[2] Later, in anger,
he tells Dr. Melliotes, "I've killed one man....I think you'll be the second."[3] He has a chance to shoot Kilbourne but instead hands the gun to
Mavis, an error since she *does* shoot her villainous husband. Even
though he knows Cathy Slocum is a murderess, Archer responds to her
feeling that she has now been, like Cain, cut off from every human being. "I understand how you feel," he says. "I was responsible, in a
way, for Pat Reavis's death."[4]

45

In *The Wycherly Woman* the woman he has been hunting tries to pay him to kill a man, assuming incorrectly that he is a hired gunman. She sees him as a kindred lost soul. He tells her that he carries a gun for protection only, but she persistently asks him if he has ever killed anyone. "Yes," he finally responds. "Eleven or twelve years ago, I killed a man named Puddler who tried to kill me."5 He wounds another vicious gunman, Frost, in the right arm and prevents Mrs. Busch from killing him in *The Barbarous Coast*. Unsuccessfully trying to protect Bess, Archer kills the murderous Una in *The Ivory Grin*. But Puddler is the killing he remembers.

In the later novels there is nothing comparable to this earlier gunplay. Archer often forgets to carry his gun, preferring to keep it locked in the trunk or glove compartment of his car. His tolerance for violence has faded considerably.

Archer is a peaceful man who cannot avoid the violence which is a natural outgrowth of the work he does. In the earlier tales Archer is badly beaten at least once during the course of each of his investigations. He is rabbitpunched and man-handled by a movie star's chauffeur-bodyguard in his very first case. Unlike Marlowe, however, he is willing to admit that violence is hazardous to his well-being.

His bruises are visible to the public. He is involved in numerous, graphically-narrated fights and beatings by gangsters. He survives being kicked in the head, having his eyes sprayed full of blue paint, being tackled by a huge deputy, and being fired upon by a Thompson submachine gun. He endures blows from saps, a poker, a tire iron, a gun butt, and brass knuckles. He is chased by a truck in *The Moving Target*, and Wilkinson's bullet puts a hole in the loose fold of a borrowed sweater in *The Zebra-Striped Hearse*.

His most flamboyant feat comes about in *The Drowning Pool* in which he and Mavis are nearly drowned in Dr. Melliotes' hydrotherapy room (a scene which was the high point of the film of the same name starring Paul Newman).

In both *Find A Victim* and *The Drowning Pool* Archer has therapeutic grudge bouts with sheriffs deranged by grief. Luckily, Archer has had boxing experience as a youngster, and Uncle Jake ("Who once went fifteen rounds with Gunboat Smith, to no decision"6) has given him a few pointers. Archer wins these battles, though Macdonald plays fair and never allows him to take on professional goons and walk away unscathed.

Archer is not above initiating physical force himself. He threatens Ronnie, Mosquito, and a treacherous desk clerk, knocks the angry artist Damis out because he is threatening with a gun, and shoots the spurious Stephen Hackett in the right leg. "If I had liked the man I might have shot to kill," he concludes ironically.7

He carries a gun more frequently in the early books, but he often finds himself unarmed in dangerous situations. He reports in *The

Name is Archer that he owns .38 and .32 calliber guns and notes that he keeps one in a locked desk drawer in his apartment and one in his office in *The Far Side of The Dollar*. He is wearing a shoulder holster which attracts Phoebe's attention in *The Wycherly Woman* and she tries to hire him as a paid killer. In *The Far Side of the Dollar* he performs "an ugly ritual" of getting his gun and harness from their drawer to impress Stella with the degree of danger involved in her situation.

When he expects armed and vicious criminals, as he assumes Leo Spillman and Professor Tappinger to be, he picks up his gun, but usually it is in his office or the back seat or trunk of the car when he most needs it. Although Archer uses his gun more than the Grogg interview might suggest, the rendition of him with gun in hand on the paperback covers of Archer books is totally misleading as a graphic portrayal of the detective's whole approach to problem solving.

Archer most often uses restraint to control the violence he faces. He trips up a knife-wielding girl in order to rescue Gretchen Keck in *The Drowning Pool*. He talks Susie Crandall out of jumping off the Golden Gate Bridge in *The Underground Man*. He is warned away from an oil spill in *Sleeping Beauty* by angry workers, then he prevents a violent outbreak between those picketing and a truck driver trying to move through them. As "the crowd began to get noisier, its groan deteriorating into a growl,"[8] Archer calmly suggests to the truck driver and Capt. Somerville that they move away at the same time urging the pickets to allow the vehicle passage. When they grumble that they don't want oil on their beaches, he responds, "It's better than blood."[9] The crowd buzzes its assent and Archer sweats in relief over violence averted.

In a similar manner he handles a threatening Mark Blackwell in *The Zebra-Striped Hearse*, and convinces Jack Lennox not to shoot. When Jack's sister disarms him, Archer observes: "Without it he looked strangely empty-handed. He was one of those men who need a gun to complete themselves."[10] Archer definitely is not one of those men. He may not be perfect, but he does not allow himself to fall into the trap of employing violence as a simple solution.

Archer is capable of showing that he cares. In *The Moving Target* he sheds tears for Alan Taggert (though supposedly Bert Graves has killed Taggert to save Archer's life). He is sick to his stomach when he sees Reavis's body in *The Drowning Pool* and again Zinnie's in *The Doomsters*. He mourns for Anne Meyer, whom he had never met. "Tears gathered behind my eyes and almost blinded me....It was anger I felt, against the helplessness of the dead and my own helplessness."[11] He also cries in anger and regret when Mrs. Wycherly's body is found.

These are not the typical responses of a hard-boiled detective. Archer has changed so much that even Macdonald himself seems to have forgotten the earlier tough guy. In the interview with *The Journal of Popular Culture*,[12] Macdonald disclosed that he himself hated guns and thus had Archer operate as much as possible without resorting to violence other than for self-defense. This modern detective has no need or use for violence.

Likewise, Archer uses very few modern gadgets and technology, and operates strictly on a low budget. He keeps an office at 8411½ Sunset Boulevard where he meets with clients and receives assorted bills and junk mail, but he spends most of his time in his car. The office is on the second floor of a two-story building with a back entrance and a private parking space. The sign on the mail-slotted door reads "Lew Archer: Private Investigator." Miss Ditmar's modeling agency is across "the rather dingy upstairs corridor" where he sees only "aspiring hopeless girls who depended on the modeling agency."[13] Both the outer room and an inner office with a one-way glass panel are small and inexpensively furnished. He has no secretary, but employs an answering service run by a discrete woman named Vera, whom he calls "a jewel."

In *The Zebra-Striped Hearse* the office is described through Mark Blackwell's eyes. His glance takes in the "drab green filing cabinet with the dents in it, the balking slats of the venetian blind, and the ugly pin-ups on the wall (and finds them) guilty as charged."[14] He questions Archer's ability to deal with prospective clients. Archer impresses no one with his affluence, or rather his lack of it.

Of Archer's many cases, only "Find the Woman," "The Sinister Habit," *The Ivory Grin*, *The Drowning Pool*, and *The Zebra-Striped Hearse* begin in this grungy setting. More often than not, Archer drives to meet a client or one catches him in court or at home. Most of his contacts are made by telephone or through the mail. Meetings in his office often place Archer in an adversary role with his clients. For instance he takes an immediate dislike to both Mrs. Dreen and J. Reginald Harlan and makes no effort to hide it. The masculine-appearing Una Durano Larkin, in blue slacks, blue mink, and a handful of rings, instantly irritates Archer at their 8:30 a.m. appointment in *The Ivory Grin*. (Eventually Archer will be forced to kill her in that office.)

The Zebra-Striped Hearse opens with a confrontation that disturbs Miss Ditmar across the hall. Archer returns from coffee to find a beautiful, wealthy-appearing woman who has come to talk to him before her husband's appointment. His mug shots on the wall—his "pin-ups," he calls them—of embezzlers, killers, bigamists, and con men, represent the kind of people he will run across in his search for the woman's step-daughter. When her indignant husband enters, Archer is forced to shield the wife from her husband's anger.

In contrast, Maude Slocum's visit has a far different effect on Archer since she is lovely and hesitant. He assures her, "Everybody hates detectives and dentists. We hate them back."[15] While Una deceives, Maude seems honest and open, and Archer, remains empathetic towards her, even after she commits suicide. Not all that happens there is productive, however. A turning point in *The Doomsters*, as well as in Archer's life, takes place when Tom Rica comes to Archer for help after seeing Alicia Hallman swimming with all her clothes on, including a mink coat. His knowledge that her death was not a suicide should have alerted the detective to prevent other murders, but Archer rejects the strange looking boy, and in despair Tom turns back to heroin. Archer's reason for snubbing the lad, is that he might have made a bad impression on a blonde he was dating. Such hypocrisy provides an unusual negative connotation to Archer's personal life.

Within the boundary of the office there is nothing much that allows the reader to learn anything about Archer's personality—no pictures other than the posters of wanted men, no art such as he admires elsewhere—and nothing of a personal nature. There is no mention of a comfortable chair (only an imitation leather sofa), nor is there even the ubiquitous bottle in the desk drawer so common in most hard-boiled dicks' digs.

In most of the novels Archer merely picks up his mail and calls in to his office. He makes short stops to collect information from the answering service, or from his co-opted colleagues.

Archer's possessions are few. He carries a contact mike in his car,[16] but rarely mentions it (he keeps his glove compartment locked, however, because the mike cost $75).[17] He keeps numerous false identification cards to aid him in obtaining inside information. A sheriff's deputy badge, an insurance adjustor's card, or a hat are the only props he needs to change personalities. He has an identity for any occasion and slips into these roles easily. To get around a suspicious maid, he "assumed my most respectable expression."[18] In the course of his travels he pretends variously to be a prop man, an exterminator, a life insurance agent, a movie talent scout, a market researcher, a hired killer, a special deputy, a wealthy editor, a personnel investigator, room service, and a journalist. The insurance and movie businesses seem to be the most useful to him. "I'm from Hollywood" always wins a respectful ear.

He assumes names with a spirit of play. After being beaten, he tells his assailants his name is "Sacher-Masoch." Cockily, he also identifies himself as "Leatherstocking" and "Natty Bumppo" (actually, the Leatherstocking *nom de plume does* seem appropriate for a specialist in tracking down men!). Cynically calling himself "S. Holmes," however, nets him nothing from the bored deputy at Citrus Junction. "Archer the wit. Archer the public relations wizard....Archer the blood hound,"[19] he scolds himself. Lesser epithets which have been applied to him are: "Goddamned truthoholic,"[20] "dirty sees-all tells-all monkey,"[21] "righteous man,"[22] "digger for facts,"[23] and "do-gooder."[24]

He is seen in different ways by different people, according to the roles he plays with them. He sometimes acts as a bearer of bad tidings, and his clients' tendencies in such cases are often to "kill the messenger."

Archer is no stranger to the Socratic method. Leonard Lister rails at "the sinister habit...the sinister habit of asking questions, as Cocteau calls it. You've got a bad case of it, Archer."25

A glance at any page of dialogue in *The Name is Archer* reveals many question marks. Archer is a prober and a wheedler of information, as a conversation with the hotel clerk in *The Ivory Grin* demonstrates. He allows the clerk to believe he is Mrs. Larkin's financial manager: "I'm looking after things for Mrs. Larkin," he declares vaguely. The clerk's question, "She isn't a Hollywood personality, by any chance?" is answered, "I'm surprised she told you."26 Then by protesting Larkin's phone bill, Archer is given the city and name of the person she called without raising the slightest suspicion.

He can convince the busiest service station manager to look up records of tire sales with his directness, or he can prompt a high school girl to tell him her darkest secrets by showing a fatherly concern. When he does ask a "bad" question, he is the first to realize it. "Where can I put my hands on her?" he asks a beautician. "It was a bad choice of expression. Her pouched eyes went over me coldly, including my hands."27 Anyone asking for Fawn King in Marie's *Salon de Paris* should know better than to phrase his question in those terms! He is given to self-deprecation. In *The Chill* Madge Gerhardi asks three questions and Archer thinks to himself, "She was stealing my lines."28

Archer's profession, however, is always based on the need to ask questions which are sometimes answered, sometimes not. He declares to the Hillmans in exasperation: "Trying to get information out of you people is like getting blood out of a stone."29

Once he has won his deliberately sought-after rapport, however, he doesn't hesitate to follow up with even more leading questions. When he reenters Susanna Drew's life she asks: "You're *not* just putting on an act, are you? To try and pry out my personal secrets, I mean."30 Jean Broadhurst observes dryly, "You're quite inquisitive, aren't you, Mr. Archer?" "It's my working habit," he answers, then continues his questioning. Later she complains, "All you do is ask questions." "I get tired of it, too," Archer replies. "Sometimes people tell me things without being asked, but you're not one of them."31

Even that statement is an implied question. Joy Rawlins says, "You're pumping me, aren't you? And I'm talking too much."32 In *Sleeping Beauty* Elizabeth Somerville wonders, "Don't you ever get tired of asking questions?"33 He answers that he *is* tired, but would rather ask than have to answer. In *The Blue Hammer* he becomes involved with Betty Jo Siddon, a newspaper woman who shares his passion for digging out the truth.

Archer works hard, asking the right questions, taking physical beatings, going without pay, being insulted by those who look down on his profession—and remaining as objective as he can through it all. When everything points to Burke Damis as the murderer in *The Zebra-Striped Hearse*, Archer notes, "In spite of the evidence tightening around him, I was trying to keep an open mind."[34]

Archer can be intensely intuitive. In "Find the Woman," he gazes into the ocean: "I felt the old primitive terror and fascination."[35] He recognizes Mrs. Dreen with that basic force: "Her eyes were green and inconstant like the sea. They said what the hell." She is "The female spider who eats her mate."[36] Intuitively, he knows she is capable of vicious actions and is jealous of her beautiful starlet daughter. He knows also that Hilda Karp is a good, trustworthy woman and that Terry Neville is self-centered, and superficial, but no killer. He acts compassionately in the face of grief, chivalrously covering the body with his own blanket. And he knows Lt. Harris was responsible for Una's death, though it takes questioning and logic to get the proof he needs.

Time and again Archer's gut level responses lead him to the truth. In "Wild Goose Chase" he sees a sad lady with eyes that are tragic and opaque, and he instinctively knows he is looking at a human being who has been used as a weapon to kill others. Though Rhea Harvey confesses, he knows how and why Glenway Cave arranged for her to do his work. All he can do is face the murderer with his moral guilt, since he is beyond the law's reach. When Cave dies in his new Ferrari, paid for through his crime, poetic justice triumphs.

As soon as he enters the case in *The Moving Target*, Archer intuits the triangle that will lead to trouble. Albert Graves sees Miranda as money, youth, and beauty; Miranda loves Alan Taggert, who has no interest in her, and Archer feels sympathy for each of the three. He also finds himself in the middle of his first family in conflict, embarrassed but prepared for violence. When he finds the body in the limousine, he's not really surprised: "I'd been feeling death in my bones for twenty-four hours."[37] Bert Graves makes the error of underestimating Archer. "Don't try to be brilliant, Lew. You never were too strong on intuition."[38] But Bert is wrong, and Archer uncovers his crime.

Archer assesses people's character traits quite easily. When he first sees James Slocum in *The Drowning Pool*, he notes that he looks "as pretty as his picture" and identifies him as gay. He takes an instant dislike to Una Durano well before he learns of her gangster affiliations. His attitude and condescension toward the black girl, Lucy, are clues that he considers her no innocent client. Isobel Blackwell says, "You're quick at catching moods"[39] when he identifies her despair as soon as she enters his office. When he sees Ronny drive off with his father and the strange young girl in *The Underground Man*, he feels a pang of dull fear for the boy and an impulse to stop Broadhurst. He doesn't, but his feelings prophesy trouble all the same.

One of Lew's leads in *The Galton Case* comes as he reads Anthony Galton's poem. He says he hates coincidences but describes his recognition of the importance of Luna as a "delayed gestalt."40 Laurel Russo's disappearance doesn't feel like a kidnapping to him, though he doesn't quite know what it is. This intuition makes sense when he connects the current episode with one when she was a teenager. Later he fits Allie Russo's death with the series of crimes going on: "I've got a feeling in my bones that her death was the beginning of all this present trouble."41

Nobody believes him at first, but he follows his intuition until he has pieced the puzzle together. The same intuition helps him solve his final case in *The Blue Hammer*. Though William Mead was murdered thirty years previous to the painting's disappearance, Archer again feels in his bones that the man responsible for that death is still alive.

It takes a special brand of intellect to unlock the mysteries of the past, and Archer's intuition enables him to succeed where other investigators have given up. It takes the added dimension of concern for people and justice to solve such deeply rooted crimes.

Although he intuits such things as fear and death, he often gets his more mundane information from eavesdropping. In fact, he is more often a "private ear" than a "private eye." At times, particularly in the earlier books, the detective deliberately places himself so that he can overhear conversations.

In *The Drowning Pool* he arrives at Maude Slocum's party early, and hearing voices on the veranda, strategically places a chair against the wall where the heavy drapes and partially closed blind conceal him. Thus he learns that Cathy and her father are more like lovers than father and daughter and that she sees herself as a bone of contention for her parents to fight over like dogs.

In *The Ivory Grin* he sidles into the booth next to Max Heiss and Dr. Benning's receptionist. He presses his ear to the plywood, straightening up quickly when Mrs. Benning storms in to scold Florie for talking to a "dirty snooper." He quietly observes as Bess breaks down Dr. Benning with her shrewishness.

Later he climbs a gate leading in to a huge Spanish-style estate which reminds him of the Inquisition. He sneaks up and stands on tiptoes, then moves to the top of a rusted, teetering table to peek in the window to watch the grotesque ritual required to keep Leo Durano calm.

In *Find A Victim* he walks through wet grass, steps over a low wall, jumps up to the front veranda, and hides in a corner against the wall, out of sight of the street. The Kerrigans are too busy arguing to pay any attention to Lew and the dying man for whom he is seeking help. He watches a fight that embarrasses him in its cruelty, and explains some of the problems that he has been encountering.

In *The Barbarous Coast* Archer enters Hester's Manor Crest Drive fortress by sneaking in the back and breaking in through a French door on the patio. Hiding in the dining room shadows, he overhears enough to let him know two killings have occurred. After he finds Lance Leonard dead, he returns and enters the house once more to catch Hester by surprise.

In *The Wycherly Woman* he attaches his contact mike to Ben Merriman's sliding glass door. Lying full length on the flagstones with his head resting on the doorsill, he learns the usual hidden inside information which could never be willingly dredged out of these hostile witnesses.

In *The Zebra-Striped Hearse* the Wilkinsons are having an argument that carries so well that he can stand outside the door and listen. Only when the argument ends does he knock.

He even listens to a conversation between Tom Hillman and the housekeeper about a previously happy, undivided family in *The Far Side of the Dollar*. Tom benefits from knowing that there are good families, and the detective realizes that if he interrupts too soon, Mrs. Perez will stop telling the story.

In *The Goodbye Look*, noting that Louise Swain's company has arrived in a suspicious-looking car, Archer takes out his trusty mike and goes around to the side of the cottage to eavesdrop. The ensuing argument carries clearly; once again what he learns changes the way he looks at the investigation.

Thus, although his communicative skills figure greatly in these tales, and although Archer is well-skilled at questioning and encouraging confession, he also takes part in a great deal of surreptitious listening. This technique keeps us privy to conversations and information we would normally not hear, and the device maintains Archer's control as an omniscient figure in the novels.

Archer's reputation for success precedes him. In *The Moving Target*, Graves, with whom he had worked in 1940-41, recommends him to the Sampsons on the basis of his skill in finding people. In *The Drowning Pool* he is recommended by "a man who does police work. He said you were honest, and discreet."[42] Archer remarks that it's strange that a policeman would say such a thing.

Leroy Frost, head of Helio-Graff's private police, indicates that he knows Archer's reputation as a smart detective, and warns him that knowing too much can get him into trouble. "You got a reputation for discretion. Use it."[43] Joshua Severn, a crime writer, is excited to meet *the* Lew Archer. Miranda Sampson is so impressed by his work that she recommends him to Keith Dalling, who, in turn, recommends him to Mrs. Lawrence in *The Way Some People Die*. Lt. Gary goes so far as to give a little speech on Archer's reputation:

I've been checking your record, as a matter of fact. A
pretty good record, as records go, in your job, in this
town. I can't say you've ever cooperated very freely,
but you've never tried to cheat us, and that's something. Also, I've talked to Colton on the D.A.'s staff
about you. He's in your corner, one-hundred per-
cent.[44]

In *The Galton Case*, in which a great amount of discretion is
mandated by the nature of the search and the wealth of the Galton family, Gordon Sable, a friend whom Archer has not seen for four years,
vouches for him "absolutely....In addition to which," Dr. Howell continues, "you have the marks of honesty on your face."[45]

Sheriff Hooper recommends him to Homer Wycherly for his
reputation for discretion again. Peter Colton also makes a recommendation to Mark Blackwell, who says, "I was told that you run one of
the best one-man operations in Los Angeles County." Blackwell adds,
"He assured me I couldn't find a better man."[46]

Conversely, Sheriff Trask accuses Lew of irresponsibility and
Archer admits error in the way he handled a witness. Trask adds, how-
ever, that "Howell came around asking me to check your record with
L.A....If you ever conned any old ladies, you never got caught."[47]

Archer's reputation is built on approval from Colton and the
Los Angeles Police Department. At the end of the novel Sable admits
that they needed to have someone they could trust to find Galton. If
they could fool Archer, they could fool anyone. If they could not, they
would try to bribe him. Sable says, "You surprise me, Lew. I didn't
expect you to bear down so hard. You have a reputation for tempering
the wind to the shorn lamb."[48] Archer has little patience though, for
ex-friends who try to manipulate him.

In *The Chill* Alex Kincaid picks Archer because his testimony
in the Perrine case indicates that he has had lots of experience. In *The
Far Side of The Dollar* Lt. Bastion says that L.A. gives him a good
rating. John Truttwell recommends him in *The Goodbye Look*, though
Mrs. Chalmers thinks he is too young and works on a shoestring.

Although Archer appreciates recommendations for the kind of
work he does, in *The Blue Hammer* he asks Betty not to print his name
because he wants to maintain his privacy. Macdonald has established
Archer as a genuine working detective with all the skills and realities of
the trade as an integral part of his character. Before Archer can function as a humanist priest he must be a competent detective.

VII.

JUDGMENT DAY

I have moral certainty and your own implicit confession.

—*The Moving Target*

    The hard-boiled hero has a passion for justice. He is known as the one who always gets his man and shows no mercy for the criminal, even if, as in the case of *The Maltese Falcon*, the detective has become romantically involved with her. The mantle of judge often descends upon him.

    It is not therefore surprising that among the hard-boiled school are men with names like Mickey Spillain's Mike Hammer and Tiger Mann, Don Pendleton's Executioner, Richard Sapir and Warren Murphy's The Destroyer, and Jon Messman's Revenger, along with the single-minded cop or sharp-shooting vigilante popularized in films by Clint Eastwood and Charles Bronson. Justice is theirs. These figures, however, are dealing with thoroughly bad criminals, the Mafia, corrupt officials, or the morally depraved.

    The early crimes Archer solves are indeed related to Chicago and Las Vegas gangsterdom, but ordinary civilians have also become involved with the murders. Although *The Moving Target*, *The Drowning Pool*, *The Way Some People Die*, *The Ivory Grin*, and *The Barbarous Coast* all include a cast of truly vicious underworld figures, the actual crimes are perpetrated by ordinary people with ordinary motives—passion, fear, jealousy, and self-preservation. They are not part of a callous army of professional killers. At times, like Graves and Sable, they are actually personal acquaintances of the victims, and are supposedly on the side of law and order themselves.

    In addition, the gangsters involved in these scenarios, such as Leo Durano of *The Ivory Grin* and Leo Ketchel of *Black Money*, can only be seen as pitiable figures. In these instances, the bad guys are "red herrings," and the detectives should sense their innocence. Many of Archer's cases feature a "mock" solution in the middle of the investigation. Then Archer must seek out "justice" in order to confront the real killer with his or her guilt.

Archer often serves as a kind of arbiter, ministering to both the guilty and the innocent. His role as judge is not limited simply to locking the criminal up or shooting him down, and over the years Archer's criminals have given way to ordinary people suffering from extraordinary errors in judgment.

"Find the Woman" sets the tone for these later works, when Archer finds a whole chain of circumstances leading to Una Sand's murder. He confronts Mrs. Dreen with his conclusion that she drove a man to such fury that he forced his wife to drown. Since she is Archer's client, and her guilt would be difficult to prove in any case, he leaves her with the dilemma of how her son-in-law will respond when he discovers he has been used as a murder weapon. Her guilt is pointed out to her, but Archer does not condemn her.

Judgment can take place in unique ways. A number of attractive women become tainted by the ugliness hidden by their guilt. Just as depicted in Oscar Wilde's classic fantasy, *The Picture of Dorian Gray*, outer physical decay can indeed be indicative of the moral decay lying just beneath the surface. Sarah Turner, the admiral's unfaithful wife, alters before Archer's very eyes as her role in his friend's death is divulged. "All day her face had been going to pieces, and now it was old and slack and ugly." Her lipstick looked "like a rim of cracked dry blood."[1]

In "The Suicide" Clare seems less attractive when she thinks of her sister's husband. After she has been struck by a gangster whom she and her sister had cheated, Archer notes: "I thought how very little it took to break a young girl down into a tramp, if she was vulnerable, or twist her into something worse than a tramp."[2] Though still young, Ethel looks like "an aged wreck of a woman."[3] Knowing there is no hope for her, Archer turns away to enable her to take her own life.

Even gorgeous women can seem ugly when their guilt is uncovered. Although Galley Lawrence is particularly lovely to look at—when she is at her most murderous, her face narrows and lengthens until she becomes "a terrible thing."[4] Bess in *The Ivory Grin* also undergoes a horrible (but typical) transformation:

> Her past was coming out on her face like latent handwriting. Her powder and lipstick, alkali and orange in the flourescent light, were cracking and peeling off. Grime showed in the pores of her nose and at the sides of her neck. Dissolution was working in her rapidly like a fatal disease she had caught from her husband that day.
>
> She felt my look cold against her, and reached up automatically to straighten her hair. It was streaked greenish yellow and black.[5]

Francine Chantry, after covering up multitudinous murders, loses her patrician beauty, with the guilty knowledge "reaching up for her from the earth like gravity."[6] The fact that they realize someone like Archer is able to see through their beauty to the ugliness of their crimes is often judgment enough for these women.

Guilt has much the same effect on men. In *The Moving Target* Graves begins to look "heavy and old"[7] after murdering Sampson. The first time Archer meets Professor Tappinger, he appears worn down. "He had probably been handsome, too, with his sensitive mouth and clean features. But he looked as if he had had a recent illness, and the eyes behind his reading glasses were haunted by the memory of it."[8]

Archer's intuition and his own moral code affect the way he looks at people. Since guilt and fear of discovery can transform the most beautiful person into an ugly one, Archer's most effective method of meting out justice includes forcing criminals to appear as corrupt on the outside as they are on the inside.

Several times Archer allows his subjects to punish themselves, as Ethel does in "The Suicide." In *The Wycherly Woman* he moves Trevor's digitalis tablets nearer to him in exchange for the man's written confession. In *The Zebra-Striped Hearse* Archer backs into the bathroom and closes the door as ordered so that Mark Blackwell can shoot himself. The severely troubled Tappinger escapes from formal justice at the end of *Black Money*, and Archer leaves to check on Laurel, allowing Marian Lennox just enough time to jump to her death. In each case these are people with guilt-ridden consciences who have already experienced punishment far worse than any formal retribution could exact.

As we have seen, Archer does not always turn criminals over to the police. When he understands the part Bert Graves has played in the murder of Sampson, he holds his tongue in front of the police. Instead, as the two of them drive to Santa Teresa, Archer confronts Graves with his suspicions.

Archer the idealist, however, is angry: "'You were the one man I thought I could trust' I couldn't find the words to end the sentence."[9] Bert has minimized the murder because Sampson was no great loss, and besides, Archer has no concrete proof to back up his accusation. Gradually, however, Bert acknowledges his feelings of guilt; then confesses to the police. At no point does Archer seem to feel a personal danger because he knows that Bert was driven to the killings by a desperate need to fulfill his desire for wealth, beauty, and youth. Bert, like Jay Gatsby, is the victim of an unattainable dream.

Archer can be merciful. In *The Drowning Pool* Archer does not tell Slocum that his wife was driven to suicide because he has no wish to see him slip even further into unreality. After confronting Cathy with her guilt and fighting Knudson to dissipate his grief, Archer allows the two of them to go back to Chicago to start a new life as father and daughter. His experience tells him that justice has been served, and his intuition suggests that Cathy will now be able to straighten out her life.

Archer lets Harriet Blackwell grieve briefly in Mexico, but he also lets her know that he is aware that she, not her father, is the murderer. Ultimately, she makes the decision to return for prosecution. At the conclusion of *Find A Victim* Hilda Church is appropriately institutionalized rather than incarcerated. In *Sleeping Beauty* Archer realizes that Somerville already has been severely punished for the infidelity that led to Allie Russo's death and that the oil spill is still connected in his mind to the fire that ruined his naval career. Archer also feels pity for the pathetic murderer at the end of *The Blue Hammer*.

Those Archer does not deign to pity are dopesters and gangsters, and people who cynically abuse others: the dope peddler who is killed by a hit-and-run accident; Dowser, whom he tricks into the police's hands; Cave, who is killed in his ill-gotten Ferrari; and Una Durano, whom he is forced to shoot.

When we first meet him, Archer appears to be put off when confronted by gays. He sees Hillary Todd (the art shop owner in "The Bearded Lady") as artificially pretty, though muscular, and observes: "Some of the ballet boys were strong and could be dangerous."10 He takes an instant dislike to James Slocum and Una Durano, and he even goes so far as to disapprove of Terry Neville's plucked eyebrows.

In his later work, however, we find Archer defending Fred Johnson from Captain Mackendrick's accusation of theft saying, "It's true, Fred could be bisexual. But I've spent a fair amount of time with him now, and haven't seen any evidence of it. *Even if he is, it doesn't make him a thief*" [my italics].11 Archer expresses no disapproval whatsoever of Paul Grimes or of the gay couple he meets at Mrs. Chantry's party. Macdonald's early use of homosexuals as villains may be a logical extension of the Philip Marlowe school of "tough-guy" homophobia. As Archer's duties become more "priestly" in nature, however, such prejudices seem to melt away.

The biases that remain are those against drug profiteers and professional criminals, evidenced by his tendency to chide those known to be "outside the law." On being offered a job by Hendryx he announces, "Forget it. I'm pretty choosy about the people I work for."12 When he observes Dowser's opulent lifestyle, he wants to deprive the gangster of those things he had gained by cheating and killing—and Archer succeeds. In the early works this attitude towards criminals takes its toll in beatings and muggings. He does not mourn Otto Sipe and Mike Harley, amateur crooks, because "They were heavy thieves, and they came to a heavy end."13

Interestingly, when he considers a person to be "evil," he won't answer to his given name of "Lew." In *The Moving Target* he tells an ex-friend, "We'll make it Mr. Archer from now on."14 At the end of *The Barbarous Coast* he is left unmoved by Leroy Frost's dying of cancer, and even tells him he belongs in a cell. "You keep calling me Lew. Don't do it," he growls.[15]

Drugs and drug pushers are anathema to Archer. In *The Moving Target*, *Find A Victim*, and *The Way Some People Die* drug use figures heavily. Betty Fraley and her brother, Eddie Lassiter, are ruined by drug abuse in *The Moving Target*. Betty is a snowbird who, in spite of spending two years in a cell without her precious piano, cannot find the strength to stop using drugs. In *Find A Victim* Lew is on his way to Sacramento to report his findings on drug distribution in the southern counties. He uses marijuana as bait in an attempt to get information from a depraved and sneaky young woman who was once a nice girl. In both books Archer is beaten after talking with drug-dependent women.

Archer has utter contempt for those who sell drugs and pity for those caught by them. Macdonald's use of drug abuse as a metaphor for social decay is intentionally emphasized. In *The Way Some People Die* Archer runs into two very young and very low criminals who entrap men the girl picks up. Arms pitted by needle marks, Ruth admits to an expensive habit. Archer dislikes her partner, Ronnie, whom she adores. "He'd started her on heroin, given her yellow fever and white death, so she was crazy about him."[16]

Archer would like to hit him, but sees no point in that or in trying to change him: sardonically he figures that Ronnie's future is "in Folsom or a mortuary or a house with a swimming pool on top of a hill."[17]

The young people tell him to look for the distributor, Mosquito, at "The Den," where he finds the piano player helpful, but also on drugs. "He had the sad bad centerless eyes I expected, wormholes in a withered appple with a dark rotten core."[18] Archer infuriates him by wasting "good" heroin, uses him to find Speed, the major dealer, and sends him for a long walk leading to his death. Archer judges drug dealers harshly.

In *The Moving Target* Archer succinctly answers Miranda's question, "Do you judge people?" with: "Everybody I meet."[19] That's his job: observing—and judging. And in his world the potential for doing evil exists in everyone. The world has definitely fallen. The war and inflation, he suggests, have helped to create "bad" people.

He finds other things to blame as well: "Environment, opportunity, economic pressure, a piece of bad luck, a wrong friend."[20] When he finds he has misjudged Graves, he is at first angry with himself, then disappointed. But his faith in Bert's basic integrity is justified when the lawyer confesses. "He was too honest to bluff it through. If nobody had suspected him, he might have. Anyone's honesty has its conditions. But he knew that I knew."[21]

This is typical of the effect Archer has on the murderers with whom he deals. He may sympathize with those who have deluded themselves into their actions, but they know he cannot be shaken once he is sure of his case.

Archer is able to reprimand the people he deals with as no one else can. When he finds that Mrs. Blackwell has been manipulating him and others, he tells her that he does not like people who play God. In *Black Money* he scolds Kitty: "What you do to other people you do to yourself—that's the converse of the Golden Rule."[22] Archer convinces Mrs. Somerville to change from her mink into a plain cloth coat with one disapproving look.[23]

Surprisingly, most of the people he chides don't stop liking him. A few, however, prove to be hopeless causes. Mr. Harley, a religious fanatic who has warped his sons, strikes Archer as being a cohort of the devil he accuses others of being in league with.[24] Lew wastes no time arguing with such obviously unbalanced people.

Still identifying heavily with the police, Archer plays fair with them far more consistently than do most "hard-boiled" detectives. Though he argues with, and, on occasion, even insults the police, only in *The Wycherly Woman* does he knowingly withhold information, thus putting himself in jeopardy of being accused of the murder.

On the other hand, he advises a policeman on how best to do his job in *The Moving Target*, giving instructions on how to handle the letters as evidence, tail a suspect, and manage a stake-out. He refuses to pick a lock in "The Sinister Habit" because he has no wish to lose his license. Archer is not about to undercut the formal machinery of justice, and because he is honest, above-board, and a good witness in a trial, he remains a favorite with defense lawyers and district attorneys alike.

He usually asks his clients initially why they haven't gone to the police first. In *The Moving Target* Mrs. Sampson says she has heard that he is good at finding people, and he replies: "`Missing Persons' is better."[25] Graves, when asked the same question responds that Sampson had often disappeared of his own accord. When kidnapping appears to be a certainty, however, following the discovery of Lassiter's body, Archer instructs Graves to contact the local police, the Los Angeles police, the sheriff, the highway patrol and the F.B.I!

During a run-in with a deputy sheriff Archer calls him "officer," even while threatening the man if he continues to treat him like a criminal. Fortunately, he succeeds in out-talking the deputy, who holds no grudge. He tells Mr. Bassett of *The Barbarous Coast* to let the police take care of pesky George Wall and his threats. When Tony complains that the county police are never around when needed, Archer counters with: "They're usually there, Tony."[26]

Archer tells Mrs. Lawrence to have Missing Persons look for Galley rather than waste her money hiring him; they work free and he charges $50 a day plus expenses. Although he does not like Brand Church, he gives him the benefit of the doubt and comes to pity him in *Find A Victim*. He also endures Sheriff Ostervelt, the corrupt old lawman at whom he snaps, "It takes more than a Colt revolver to change a Keystone Kop into an officer."[27]

Still Archer continues to have faith in the legal system, and as he expresses it in *The Name is Archer*: "Very few innocent men are convicted of murder."[28] Even in *The Wycherly Woman*, in which he does some questionable things to get at the truth, he advises using the police, "a national detective agency, mass-media publicity, all-out police dragnet, with FBI cooperation, if possible"[29] in order to solve the case.

Archer is neither arrogant nor over-confident. He has a greater loyalty to serving his clients and finding the truth than he has need to build up his own ego or reputation. In spite of a disillusioning experience as a policeman and his awareness that corruption exists, Archer comes down hard on the side of the formal agencies of justice. As a judge of people who commit crimes, he operates well within the existing legal system, representing and upholding the society to which he ministers.

VIII.

THROUGH A MIRROR DARKLY

*For an instant I was the man in the mirror, the
shadow-figure without a life of his own who peered
with one large eye and one small eye through dirty
glass at the lives of people in a very dirty world.*
—*The Drowning Pool*

Archer is not really a "hero" in the sense of being an ideal in
all things, but he is the catalyst which provides the final resolution of
the problem at hand, and he often takes an active role in the rehabilita-
tion process set in motion at the end of the story. He is intensely introspective, and spends much of his time remembering the past, thinking
about himself, and telling others about his experiences. He is not proud
of everything he has had to do to solve crimes. He is a decent person
albeit a very human one—a flawed saint.

In *Sleeping Beauty* he mentally fills in a registration card:
"Lew Archer: thief catcher, corpse finder, ear to anyone."[1]

Archer is self-analytical. In *The Blue Hammer* he is drawn to
the charismatic leader of the Society of Mutual Love. While the
Biemeyer girl and Fred Johnson go with the sheriff, Archer stays behind to talk:

"You seem to be a man engaged in an endless
battle, an endless search. Has it ever occurred to you
that the search may be for yourself? And that the way
to find yourself is to be still and silent, silent and
still?" He dropped his arms to his sides.

I was tired enough to be taken by his questions,
and to find myself repeating them in my mind. They
were questions I had asked myself, though never in
just those terms. Perhaps, after all, the truth I was
looking for couldn't be found in the world. You had
to go up on a mountain and wait for it, or find it in
yourself.[2]

Back in his hotel room Archer comforts the sobbing thirty-two-year-old who feels his life is ruined. He had hunted for Mildred Mead because he felt she was the source of Doris' family problems and the key to solving them. Archer thinks to himself:

> Like other lost and foolish souls, Fred had an urge to help people, to give them psychotherapy even if it wrecked them. When he was probably the one who needed it most. Watch it, I said to myself, or you'll be trying to help Fred in that way. Take a look at your own life, Archer.
> But I preferred not to. My chosen study was other men, hunted men in rented rooms, aging boys clutching at manhood before night fell and they grew suddenly old. If you were the therapist, how could you need therapy? If you were the hunter, you couldn't be hunted. Or could you?[3]

Archer looks at himself—literally—by studying his face in mirrors. In *The Moving Target* the mirror scene is quite pointedly an introduction to the hero. Archer has picked up the drunken actress, Fay Estabrook, in hopes of finding Sampson. He feels guilty, and even refers to himself as a gigolo, for using the lady in this way. The description elicited in this scene tells us a great deal about the Archer of all the novels.

> I looked at my face in the mirror and didn't like it too well. It was getting thin and predatory-looking. My nose was too narrow, my ears were too close to my head. My eyelids were the kind that overlapped at the outside corners and made my eyes look triangular in a way that I usually liked. Tonight my eyes were like tiny stone wedges hammered between the lids.[4]

Mystery readers may recall that Sam Spade's physical description is also given in triangular terms. Spade, however, was never so self-critical, so given to analyzing his own motives. Archer knows here that he is playing a role, a difficult job at which most detectives excel.

> I tried smiling to encourage myself. I was a good Joe after all. Consorter with roughnecks, tarts, hard cases and easy marks: private eye at the keyhole of illicit bedrooms; informer to jealousy, rat behind the walls, hired gun to anybody with fifty dollars a day; but a good Joe after all. The wrinkles formed at the corners of my eyes, the wings of my nose, the lips drew

back from the teeth, but there was no smile. All I got was a lean famished look like a coyote's sneer. The face had seen too many bars, too many rundown hotels and crummy love nests, too many courtrooms and prisons, post-mortems and police lineups, too many nerve ends showing like tortured worms. If I found the face on a stranger, I wouldn't trust it.[5]

This passage illustrates how Archer feels about what he does. He knows he needs to find the truth and put the pieces together, but he also sees himself as a scavenger who cleans up society's garbage: "Most of my work is divorce. I'm a jackal, you see."[6]

This ambivalence leads Archer to be very sensitive to what others say and think about his profession. When he is treated as though he were part and parcel of the people he deals with, he either lashes out or makes wisecracks about his "subprofession." He is furious with Ralph Smitheram for calling him a "junior G-man." He is offended when someone else suggests that he could "do better."

Archer is further reflected most tellingly in Gretchen Keck's warped mirror in *The Drowning Pool*:

The man in the mirror was big and flat-bodied, and lean-faced. One of his gray eyes was larger than the other, and it swelled and wavered like the eye of conscience: and the other eye was little, hard and shrewd. I stood still for an instant, caught by my own distorted face, and the room reversed itself like a trick drawing in a psychological test. For an instant I was the man in the mirror, the shadow-figure without a life of his own who peered with one large eye and one small eye through dirty glass at the lives of people in a very dirty world.[7]

Here we have one of the most vivid and, perhaps, one of the most disturbing visions of the "private eye" in hard-boiled literature. Distorted as this image may seem, however, it remains an accurate portrait of the modern literary detective. The "eye of conscience" is the defender of moral order while the "eye of shrewdness" is the practical skill any detective must possess to unearth the truth. The "shadow-figure" (the detective who becomes invisible when he turns sideways) moves in to solve a crime, then moves out of human contact once again. He represents the detective's alter-ego—the distancing agent which serves to isolate and protect the detective from becoming too closely involved in his cases.

Archer minimizes his own self-interest as he quietly goes about his work, telling little about himself, unless it can be used as an object lesson, and serving as an abstraction of justice, like the paintings he sees in the homes of the wealthy.

Other mirror images appear in *The Galton Case* as Archer tries to avoid looking in a mirror after a severe beating. "One of my front teeth was broken off short. My nose resembled a boiled potato."[8] He is so angry at the sight that he attacks his assailant but fails, mentally drafting a letter restricting the manufacture of guns to military use.

After being struck with a tire iron in *The Wycherly Woman*, he observes that "I looked like an Indian holy man who had run out of holiness and just about everything else."[9] As he shaves with a razor borrowed from Deputy Mungan in *The Zebra-Striped Hearse*, Archer says, "All I uncovered was the same old trouble-prone face."[10]

And then there is the image Archer faces in *The Goodbye Look*, in which he identifies with Sidney Harrow, a man who represents all the seamy things a detective can run across in his work. The same unpleasant feeling is unleashed in *The Instant Enemy* as Archer thinks about the corrupt and sneaky Jack Fleischer. "Facing him in the semi-darkness, I had the feeling that I was looking at myself in *a bleared, distorting mirror*." [my emphasis][11] Archer sees traces of himself in this man who had been manuevered into covering up a crime with his police power.

A different kind of image is presented by Ward Rasmussen, a capable and dedicated young patrolman who wants to become a detective. Archer is attracted to him immediately:

> My heart went out to the boy. More than twenty years ago, when I was a rookie on the Long Beach force, I had felt very much as he did. He was new to the harness, and I hoped it wouldn't cut too deep into his willing spirit.[12]

Just as Ward represents the idealistic young Archer, Tom Rica mirrors his "bad" side. In *The Doomsters* Archer sees in the lad reflections of the mistakes in human relations that led not only to his breakup with Sue, but will end with his failure to save Tom from the drug addiction that has entrapped him.

Archer's introspectiveness can cause him to be quite hard on himself. In *The Name is Archer* he blames himself for his "famous quick decisions, the kind you wake up to in the middle of the night reconsidering five years later."[13]

He thinks of himself as "trouble looking for a place to happen."[14] When Hester calls him a "sadist" in *The Barbarous Coast*, he begins to doubt his own motives, aware that there may very well be a streak of cruelty in his drive to bring about justice.

He is very uncomfortable around the desirable Mildred in *The Doomsters* and worriedly compares his "quasi-paternal instinct" to Ostervelt's forthright lust. He can visualize himself as a middle-aged Lothario chasing a beautiful young woman when he takes the troubled Laurel Russo home with him.

He constantly evaluates himself in this unflattering manner, noting his bad handling of people, oafish remarks, poor questions, and ill-timed witticisms.

He disgusts himself when he finds it necessary to harass witnesses. "I was a great hand at frightening boys,"[15] he thinks as he drags information from the punk Ronnie. As he questions Stella in *The Far Side of the Dollar*, he gets "a sudden evil image of myself: a heavy hunched figure seen from above in the act of tormenting a child who was already tormented."[16] Questioning Sandy in *The Instant Enemy* he has the same kind of distorted picture of himself. "I had a vision of myself seen from above, a kind of owl's-eye view of a man moving in on a frightened girl at a deserted crossroads. Somehow my motives didn't enter the picture."[17]

He is so angry at Hillman that he tells him he is sick of him and his affairs. "He was astonished. I was astonished myself. Angry shouting at witnesses is something reserved for second-rate prosecuters in courtrooms."[18] When Doris Biemeyer in *The Blue Hammer* says that he is not very nice, he very nearly agrees with her. In *The Barbarous Coast* he has doubts when Rina asks him if he is a "good man."

> "I like to think so," but her candor stopped me. "No," I said, "I'm not. I keep trying, when I remem- ber to, but it keeps getting tougher every year. Like trying to chin yourself with one hand. You can prac- tice all your life, and never make it."[19]

He is uncomfortable when he "cons" the alcoholics Fay Estabrook and Mr. Johnson by feeding them drinks in order to lull them into giving him information. Even though he is not above hitting people at their weakest points, it still eats at him.

He does not always take himself so seriously, however. In *The Galton Case* he makes fun of the broken-toothed lisp his temporary crown causes by pushing against his upper lip.[20] No matter how vicious the beating, he can still laugh at his abortive attempts to be a tough guy. This humor helps to lighten the grittiest part of the "hard-boiled" depictions.

Archer is not impervious to pain, and he occasionally lands in a hospital or at the dentist. After he brings a body in from the sea in *Sleeping Beauty*, he notes: "The wet towel hung like a cold lead apron around my loins. I was lobster red in the trunk, fish blue in the extremities."[21] He sometimes goes too far with this kind of absurdity. When his car is stolen by a man whose own vehicle has been wrecked, Archer climbs down a bank to see what he has traded for:

"I'm Captain Nemo," I said. "I just came ashore
from a hostile submarine. Curiously enough, we fuel
our subs with seaweed. The hull itself is formed from
highly compressed seaweed. So take me to your wis-
est man. There is no time to be lost."22

The deputies in charge of the wreck suspect they have a
"crazy" on their hands.

Archer is prone to innocent mistakes in his dealings with the
public. His nutty brand of humor gets him in trouble regularly. He
hurts Tom's feelings in *The Doomsters* just when this sensitive young
man needs help desperately. He infuriates the dangerous Cuddy in *The
Instant Enemy* by calling him stupid. Not learning from experience, he
does the same thing to Pennell. His good humor keeps him from re-
gretting such mistakes for long. In "Gone Girl" Archer admits,
"There's an unexplained trace of canine in my chromosomes."23

Among the many divorce cases, commitment trials, bodyguard
jobs, tails, testimonies, experiences with con men, gangsters, and mental cases Archer has handled, he remembers his failures most clearly.

On the other hand, Macdonald makes no attempt to portray
Archer as infallible. At the start of "Gone Girl" Archer is coming back
from the Mexican border where he had lost a man he had been tailing
from Fresno in Old Town's mazes. He admits to Una Durano that he
doesn't think he could find a black girl in Los Angeles. A client's wife
commits suicide during his divorce investigation, and he inadvertently
saves a notorious hustler from being convicted one of the few times she
is innocent.

In "Find the Woman" he assumes, incorrectly, that the infuriated husband drowned Una Sand. He underestimates Galley in *The
Way Some People Die*, and in *The Ivory Grin* he waits too long to contact Lucy. In *The Chill* he leaves Helen unprotected when she insists
she is going to be murdered, suspects Bradshaw of murder, but never
imagines that Bradshaw's mother and Tish are the same woman. In
Black Money he leaves Harry in his car trunk for a long time while he
runs around on other errands. Twice he misses the chance to save lives
by not taking the time to listen, first to Tom Rica in *The Doomsters*,
then to Bess Tappinger in *Black Money*.

His worst error, in *The Drowning Pool*, continues to haunt
Archer. He informs Knudson's office that he and Musselman are
bringing in Reavis, the prisoner from the Slocum case. They are
blocked by a truck pulled across the road, and half a dozen masked
gunmen. Archer is knocked cold, and Musselman watches helplessly as
the men shoot Reavis a dozen times, pour gas on him, set fire to him,
and throw him down the embankment. Seeing the charred remains of
the man he had in custody, Archer is ill.

Reavis, though an unpleasant character, did not deserve his fate, and Archer accepts full blame for it: "I remembered what I had done to Reavis, and felt a twinge of hypocrisy. Remorse and fear mixed in my veins, and made a bitter blend." Later, Archer has a dream featuring a "charred featureless face....a calcined man" approaching, "his footsteps soft as ashes."[24]

Archer's first concern is for the truth. He does not like to be forced to lie. In dredging out the address of Hester Wall's mother, Archer goes through a childish routine of "Cross my heart and hope to die" with the saleslady. "It felt like the kind of lie that would bring me bad luck. It was."[25]

In *The Way Some People Die* he slips up by not questioning Dalling more thoroughly. Instead he leaves him, gets knocked out, and Dalling is killed. Archer blames the error on the whiskey he drank and, perhaps more importantly, on his own negative feelings toward the cowardly man.

In *The Chill* Helen Haggerty's death is caused because he refused to take her seriously. His guilt becomes a "private" obsession causing Jerry Marks to observe, "This case is a personal matter with you?"[26] Dolly Kincaid's father feels betrayed by Archer when the sheriff's men arrest him after following the detective to his hiding place. Once again Archer's carelessness may have been the culprit.

That he manages to survive all this violence and mayhem is somewhat amazing. Archer goes to Kilbourne's mansion and holds a gun on his guard. He threatens to pistol-whip the old man, but hesitates, reflecting:

> I wanted to hurt him, but the memory of the night was ugly in my mind. There had to be a difference between me and the opposition, or I'd have to take the mirror out of my bathroom. It was the only mirror in the house, and I needed it for shaving.[27]

This last bit of ironical introspection cannot mask the serious doubts about his honor that Archer is feeling. And as we have seen, the mirror as symbol plays an important role in Archer's externalization of his sub-conscious self.

Archer sardonically attempts to come to terms with his ability to judge people as all good or bad in *The Doomsters*:

> It was a comforting idea, and bracing to the ego. For years I'd been using it to justify my own activities, fighting fire with fire and violence with violence, running on fool's errands while the people died: a slightly earthbound Tarzan in a slightly paranoid jungle. Landscape with figure of hairless ape.[28]

To Archer, however, his greatest lapse remains his failure to rescue Tom Rica from drug addiction. Archer eventually must acknowledge to himself that the damage is done. "The circuit of guilty time was too much like a snake with its tail in its mouth, consuming itself. If you looked too long, there'd be nothing left of it or you. We were all guilty. We had to learn to live with it."29

William Ruehlmann claims that the reasons for Archer's problem with personal guilt are quite simply: "He has lost his wife, he did not complete college, he resigned from the Long Beach force."30 These rather obvious personal problems are only superficially to blame, however. At the heart of the matter is Archer's tendency to identify with the people he meets and to equate his errors with theirs which endows his guilt with the quality of an original sin in the theological sense. *I am a man: therefore I am capable of evil.*

Most of the fictional detectives whose lineage can be traced back to Dupin—Travis McGee, Mike Hammer, Philo Vance, Perry Mason, Philip Marlowe, Sam Spade—spend little or no time developing such close bonds with their clients. And none seem to feel quite the same sense of personal failure or guilt when things go wrong as Archer does.

The traditional hard-boiled detective should be a chess player, manipulating men with no regrets. Archer, on the other hand, is not much of a game player; when he loses a man, he hurts.

A reconstruction of Archer's youthful background is difficult, but at least some of it can be pieced together from the internal evidence in the books. Lew grew up in Long Beach, was a teenaged hood, tried college but dropped out, joined the Long Beach police force and worked his way up to detective sergeant before quitting. He joined the army, served in combat, moved to Los Angeles following his discharge, set up a private detective agency—and married and divorced Sue.

His family was not well-to-do but they were proud of their heritage. His mother and grandmother were Catholics, so he's been exposed to a little Latin. He recalls his father holding his hand as he waded in the ocean at Long Beach.

An important influence on his life was his Uncle Jake. Although his mother refused to keep pictures of the man because she was ashamed of having a professional fighter in the family, Archer has extremely fond memories of him:

> I could remember the smell of him, composed of Bay
> rum, hair oil, strong clean masculine sweat and good
> tobacco and the taste of the dark chocolate cigarettes
> he brought....31

and in his fights he draws strength from the fact that he is Jake's nephew.

He was a typical rebellious teenager. In *The Doomsters* he declares, "I hadn't been so mad since the day I took the strap away from my father."[32]   His disgusted reaction to rich clients' beautiful but spoiled children suggests a more humble beginning.   He views Cathy Slocum as "one of the girls I had watched from a distance in high school and never been able to touch; the girls with oil or gold or free-flowing real-estate money dissolved in their blood like blueing."[33]

Of all of his relatives, his grandmother seems to have left the most vivid impression on him.   In *The Goodbye Look* he recalls that she "used to live with birds in the garden in Contra Costa County,"[34] and Archer himself is a great bird fancier (as was Macdonald), seeing them both in symbolical terms, and keeping them literally, like his scrub jays, as friends.

In *The Way Some People Die* the tea leaves in his cup remind him that his grandmother would have read them (he recalls that she always spoke in a whisper).   Miss Jenks' living room powerfully invokes the old-fashioned parlor in his grandmother's house in Martinez, where a hand-embroidered motto on the wall there proclaimed: "He is the Silent Listener at Every Conversation,"[35] a phrase which could describe Archer just as easily as it does the Holy Redeemer.

Her moral qualities, in fact, have had a profound influence on Lew.   In *Black Money* he says to Peter Jamieson that: "She always said it was sinful to despair,"[36] and in *The Blue Hammer* he tries to comfort Paula Grimes as she mourns her father's death in the hospital chapel. She rejects him because he is not a priest, and Archer reflects on the fact that he might very well have become a priest, had he followed his grandmother's wishes.

> There were times when I almost wished I was a priest.
> I was growing weary of other people's pain and wondered if a black suit and a white collar might serve as armor against it.   I'd never know.   My grandmother in Contra Costa County had marked me for the priesthood, but I had slipped away under the fence.[37]

In reality, perhaps, Archer has not escaped such a vocation altogether.

IX.

THE LONELY STREETS

*She said she couldn't stand the life I led. That I gave
too much to other people and not enough to her. And
I guess she was right in a way. But it really boiled
down to the fact that we weren't in love any more. At
least, one of us wasn't.*

—*Find a Victim*

The one person in Archer's life most frequently referred to
(although she never appears in person in any of the novels), is his ex-
wife, Sue. Apparently his occupation became too much for her to endure. Mrs. Kerrigan asks if he has ever felt as if he had no future or
past. He replies that he felt that way the week his wife left.[1]

Archer mourns his marriage throughout the novels. In *The
Moving Target* Graves, inquiring about Sue, is told: "Ask her lawyer.
She didn't like the company I kept."[2] He refuses to elaborate. Alone
at home, he brings in the milk, thaws out some oysters, and makes a
stew. His wife had never liked oysters, but now he is free to eat them
any time he likes. After that he undresses and gets into his bed, ig-
noring the empty twin on the other side of the room. At least, he reflects, he does not have to explain what he has been doing all day.

In *The Drowning Pool* he tells Maude Slocum that he understands her feelings about divorce since his wife had divorced him on the
grounds of mental cruelty. In *The Way Some People Die* he describes
his home in a middle-class residential section between Hollywood and
Los Angeles. "The house and the mortgage on it were mementos of my
one and only marriage. Since the divorce I never went home till sleep
was overdue."[3]

Bess, who he intuits is capable of murder, asks the usual personal questions when he tells her he is the last of his line and does not
want it to die out through drinking poisoned coffee. He tells her only
that he has no wife or children. In *The Barbarous Coast*, Archer considers contacting Mona, whom he had met at a party: "A man got
lonely in the stucco wilderness, pushing forty with no chick, no
child."[4]

The Doomsters dredges up some of the most painful memories found in the novels. Archer realizes that he had been a hero to Tom until the divorce proceedings brought out facts which were "a little worse than usual." When Tom tries to ask his advice, Lew, on the rebound from Sue, is dating a blonde who would be put off by the boy, and he rebuffs him. Tom's presence is a vivid reminder of Archer's own failures. "It seemed that my life had dwindled down to a series of one-night stands in desolate places."5

The novel ends with Archer wondering "Where she was, what she was doing, whether she'd aged much as she lay in ambush in time, or changed the color of her bright head."6 Archer spends a great deal of time feeling miserable because he has failed to sustain the one most important human relationship in his life.

Archer finds it difficult to consider replacing Sue in his life. In spite of his warmth and concern for his clients, his pain seems obvious to those around him. Mr. Wycherly thinks he understands Archer because he, too, is a divorced man. In *The Chill* Mrs. Bradshaw, a perceptive woman, asks Archer if he is married, then asks if he is Alex's father. She senses his feeling of sympathy for the young man who has lost a loved wife. When Mrs. Blackwell asks him if he has been married, he says yes, but adds that his personal life is irrelevant, a patent untruth.

Fawn King reminds him of Sue, but he claims to have forgotten her name. "There was too much pain in the word, and this was no place to deposit it." When Fawn asks about his wife, he says, "Nothing bad happened to her. She left me, but that wasn't bad for her. It was bad for me. Eventually she married somebody else and had some kids and lived happily ever after."7 Fawn assumes that Sue left because Archer cheated on her, but he swears he remained faithful (though he admits he treated her badly).

Archer can open up to women like Fawn, because they are in trouble and vulnerable themselves. He also confides in Moira Smitheram, a woman about to divorce her husband. He mentions an earlier surfing trip to San Onofre with his friends. But his wife was not interested. "She divorced me back in those same forties. I don't blame her. She wanted a settled life, and a husband she could count on to be there."8

Although he doesn't mention it, Archer empathizes with Kilpatrick in *The Underground Man*. Jerry blames his father for his parents' breakup fifteen years previous to the events of the novel. His mother, Ellen, cut off all contact, sending the divorce notice through her lawyer in Reno. The same kind of process dissolved Archer's marriage. Apparently both women shared a disapproval of their husbands' seven-day work week, the constantly ringing phones, and the caliber of the clients. Yet Archer does not mention his personal feelings to this unhappy man.

When he meets Ellen, however, he admits he is a little para-noid from living alone. "By choice?" she asks. "Not mine," he replies. "My wife couldn't live with me. But now I'm used to it."[9] They have an easy relationship not marred when Lew turns down her offer to sleep with her.

Similarly, in *Sleeping Beauty*, he sympathizes with Tom, whose wife has "disappeared" even before she is physically missing. He tells Elizabeth that Tom is a "willing man. If I had been half as willing, I could have held on to my own wife."[10] Archer *is* willing to reach out to women and comfort them by sharing his feelings of loneli-ness, but he rarely makes such admissions to the men in his cases who share a similar loss. This "machismo," perhaps, is Archer's method of maintaining his image as a rough-and-tough, hard-boiled detective.

Archer, apparently, has never recovered from the pain of los-ing Sue, even though he no longer knows where she is—or even if she is still alive. In *The Blue Hammer* the artist Simon Lashman laments his loss of the beautiful Mildred Mead who left him for another man. He blames himself, not her, for he had not treated her well. Archer thinks to himself: "His words set up a vibration in my mind. I'd had a woman and lost her, but not to another man. I'd lost her on my own."[11]

The Biemeyer quarrels remind him of those he had had with Sue. Back in Long Beach to meet Francine Chantry in "The Galleon," he recalls escaping to the bar while his marriage was disintegrating.

So much repetition of the questions, "Are you married?" or "Are you a family man?" cannot be coincidental in these tales. Archer was not unfaithful, not a wife-beater, nor was he indifferent to Sue: but he did put his obsession for the pursuit of truth ahead of her and his personal life. Details in the novels reveal that, once on a case, he rarely sleeps or returns home until he has solved the mystery at hand.

He lives, instead, cloistered in his Ford—alone on a California highway. He is too preoccupied with his role in life to allow room for anything more than temporary liaisons. He may be lonely, but he has chosen this rather celibate life-style, and its close parallel to the priestly calling precludes a personal commitment.

Sue, no doubt, had reason to be suspicious of her husband's fi-delity. Detectives are notorious for being surrounded by treacherous women and demented nymphomaniacs (like Brigid O'Shaunnessy and the Sternwood sisters), and the usual hard-boiled detective has few scruples where their female clients are concerned.

Archer's literary successor, Spenser, sleeps with a mother and her daughter on the same day in *The Godwulf Manuscript*! Archer, however, remains relatively celibate. Although attractive women are readily available to him, he rarely sleeps with any of them, and has been known to turn down even the most inviting offers.

Archer is rescued (in *The Drowning Pool*) by the gorgeous Mavis Kilbourne, who could have been a movie star had she not become her husband's property instead (her ulterior motive is to recover the pornographic film with which she is being blackmailed). She and Archer survive torture and possible drowning at the hands of her husband, whom she kills in revenge. Tempted by her beauty (not to mention her ten-million dollar inheritance), Archer nevertheless convinces her to plead self-defense rather than run off with her to South America. He has no real desire to spend his future with a larcenous, murderous ex-gun-moll.

Nor does he give in to the charms of Gretchen Keck, a seventeen-year-old, deserted by her mother and on her own working as a hooker. Still convinced she is basically a "nice" girl, he gives her the $10,000 he might have kept for himself and lies to her about Reavis' dying words to enable her to feel good about herself. In spite of his sympathy for her, Archer wants no part of this tainted young woman.

He picks up Jerry Mae (the prostitute in *Find A Victim*) who takes him to her room. He pays for her information but turns down her offer of sex. Jo Summer mistakes him for her boyfriend, and welcomes him with a passionate kiss, but after she recognizes him, she sneaks out and sets him up to be beaten and robbed. The antagonistic sheriff's wife, Hilda Church makes a desperate pass at Lew, and pleads with him to stay with her. But Archer has no desire to take advantage of these desperate women.

Kate Kerrigan is the first innocent woman to turn to Archer. Her husband, who has been involved with many other women because of her frigidity, justifies his behavior by telling her that she has never made him feel "like a man." Stung, Kate asks Archer his opinion of her. His somewhat oblique answer is that he felt like a man before he met her.

Archer resists other beautiful women. The vicious killer, Galley Lawrence, in *The Way Some People Die*, has fooled most people into seeing her as lovely and innocent. But physical beauty, especially in the hard-boiled detective's world, is not always the equivalent of goodness and decency. Archer, staring at her high school picture, comes to the conclusion that: "She must have stood out in her graduating class like a chicken hawk in a flock of pullets."[12] The image is telling. Galley is beautiful—but dangerous.

Bess Wionowski Benning in *The Ivory Grin* is similarly breathtaking. Her past, however, is checkered by the deaths of the men who once loved her, and her husband has become a monster because of the way she treats him. Accustomed to using her beauty to control men, she attempts to lure Archer without much success. He takes her head in his hands (but only to check for light roots in her dark hair to ascertain that she is Singleton's mystery blonde). Archer is not so easily seduced by corrupted beauty.

In *The Doomsters* he is, however, powerfully attracted to the lovely, petite, Mildred Hallman, whose husband is presumed to be a dangerous lunatic. His fascination with Mildred embarrasses him because he senses that both Sheriff Ostervelt and Dr. Grantland, whom he despises, are similarly attracted by her charms. She seems much too vulnerable to be subjected to three such aging wolves, and his relationship with her remains platonic. Her sister-in-law, Zinnie, repels Archer with her aggressiveness, although he finds her attractive, and becomes physically ill when her body is discovered. Staying emotionally distanced from both of these doomed women was a wise decision.

The first woman he makes love to in the novels is Ada Reicher, who had been involved with the presumed Galton heir. She is lean, attractive, intense, and intelligent. He admires her honesty and feels sorry for her loss of self-esteem after the boy dumps her. Archer finds it difficult to resist a woman who says of herself: "I'm no good. I betrayed him. Nobody could love me. *No*body could."[13] Her words anger him, but he notices her long beautiful back and decides to "comfort" her.

Stanley Quillan's friend Jessie in *The Wycherly Woman* tells Archer he's "sweet," and an obvious replacement for Stanley. Sally Merriman is another unhappy wife looking for a man to make her feel wanted again. He describes her as a "lost lady happy to be found....Her body tempted my hands, in spite of the drowned one floating behind my eyes; in spite of all the old numb burn-marks which bodies like hers had left on my nerve-ends."[14]

Archer misses the easy kind of relationship that he had hoped for when he finally finds the woman he believes is Mrs. Wycherly. She is intrigued by the thought that he is a gunman. She throws herself at him in a crude manner that shocks Archer, who had been expecting a more experienced seductress. Blaming her awkwardness on drink he notes, "I felt as though I was being offered a large and dangerous gift I didn't want. Her pointed breasts were like soft bombs against me."[15] He understands that she is miserable, but fails to see that she is only pretending to be Catherine.

In *The Chill* Archer walks away from another woman, with dire consequences. Professor Helen Haggerty is a blonde with good legs, stylish clothes, and "a restless predatory air." She waits for Archer in a parking lot where she promises him information about Dolly Kincaid. He follows her home for a drink where she announces that he is the first interesting man she has met since her arrival. The line is pretty obvious, and Archer expects that they will use each other. She explains to Lew that although her life has been threatened, the police will not take the threats seriously. Unfortunately, Archer succumbs neither to her wiles nor to her frightened plea for help. The next time he sees her, of course, she is dead.

In *Black Money* there is obviously something wrong with Mrs. Harry Hendricks, known also as Kitty Ketchel. Archer observes: "The room provided roles for only two people. I guessed what mine would be if we stayed in it much longer. Her body was purring at me like a tiger, the proverbial kind of tiger which is dangerous to mount and even more dangerous to dismount."[16] When he resists her charms, she suddenly fears that he is a hired killer from Las Vegas. But she doesn't give up easily. The next time they meet she again tries to seduce him into recovering the gangster's money for her. She is obviously not Archer's type.

Neither is Bess Tappinger, who responds all too enthusiastically to him for his comfort. The first time he sees her, although Peter is with him, she attempts to catch his attention, and he has to admit she interests him, married, or not. On his next visit, he brings pink champagne, and finds her all dressed up. "I didn't like the purposeful look in her eye, and I began to regret the pink champagne. She took it from my hands as if she planned to break it over the prow of an affair."[17] With her youngest child away at nursery school and her husband in class, she requests a ride from a suspicious Archer. Alone with him she tries to gain his sympathy, speaking of her marital frustrations and her lost youth. Archer merely listens. As a last resort, she changes into a dress that has to be hooked up in the back. Archer has a revealing conversation with himself:

> Though she had a strokable-looking back my hands were careful not to wander. The easy ones were nearly always trouble: frigid or nympho, schizy or commercial or alcoholic, sometimes all five at once. Their nicely wrapped gifts of themselves often turned out to be homemade bombs, or fudge with arsenic in it.[18]

Archer, as we know, is capable of making a fatal error in judgment. He cuts Bess off rudely when she calls to tell him "something important," by snapping that "counseling housewives whose lives are changing is not my job." When he next sees her, he has to admit to himself that he has at least considered the idea of making love to her. More importantly, however, her revelations not only explain the case, but she convinces Archer that her husband is truly dangerous. Putting her off has delayed his work, but he soothes his conscience by remembering that old adage: "Never sleep with anyone whose troubles are worse than your own."[19]

In *The Instant Enemy* physical contact with the beautiful Mrs. Sebastian results in a mutual attraction, but Archer is too busy with a complicated manhunt to be diverted. He accepts a check for $100,000 from Ruth Marburg, and she touches his cheek in a gesture of possessiveness. He snaps in response: "You bought your son with this check, not me."[20] Ruth's daughter-in-law, Gerda, also plants a kiss on him in passionate gratitude, but she is not as attractive as the other two women, and he finds it easy to say simply that he is employed by her husband and cannot make love to her in his home.

Moira Smitheram, like Ada, has lost faith in herself as a woman, and Archer does not resist her. Drawn to each other immediately, their words are soon charged with double entendre. She has married too young, and her mink coat, Cadillac convertible, and elegant house cannot possibly compensate for her preoccupied psychiatrist husband's neglect of her.

Moira and Lew take a serious and introspective look into their lives and discover that they are both lonely, middle-aged people looking for continuity in an uncertain world. Both have been hurt by past loves. Archer dislikes and suspects her husband, and thus questions his motives toward Moira. He stops himself from digging too deeply into her past because: "if I started to use the woman and the occasion, I'd be using a part of myself and my life that I tried to keep unused: the part that made the difference between me and a computer, or a spy."[21]

He does sleep with her, however, and she tells him he is a gentle lover who makes her feel, interestingly, "like Eve in the garden again."[22] They are well suited and remain close throughout the rest of the novel. But although Moira eventually leaves her husband, she decides not to continue her relationship with Archer. Lew's attention to her restored her self-confidence enough for her to make a long-delayed change, but her relationship with him was not responsible for the breakup of her marriage. A woman associated with a crime Archer is investigating usually has no chance of continuing a meaningful relationship with him.

The Underground Man begins with Archer's affection for both little Ronny Broadhurst, and his pretty young mother, Jean. Archer adopts them as a kind of surrogate family, and maintains a warm relationship with the girl, without the usual sexual overtones. Although Jean offers casual sex, she is not overly upset when Lew rejects her invitation. Handsome Ellen Broadhurst (more his type) offers to share her bed for the night, but Archer is too concerned that Ellen might be involved in the case at hand to reciprocate.

He doesn't wait for an offer from Elizabeth Somerville in *Sleeping Beauty*. She, like Moira, has a husband whose interests lie elsewhere, and Archer can't help but confiding to her his own marital woes. He is strongly attracted to her physically:

> Touched by emotion, her back was beautiful. The narrow waist blossomed out into strong hips, which narrowed down again into a fine pair of legs.[23]

Once more a woman's beauty, combined with despair and feelings of failure, lead Archer to her bed. But the next day a body is discovered nearby in the ocean, and the spell is broken. Elizabeth has become a part of Archer's larger mystery—and they part:

> I bade a silent farewell to her narrow-waisted back.
> The night before had been a one-time thing, not with-
> out passion but without consequences. Except that I
> would never forget Elizabeth.[24]

(A note might be made here about Archer's fascination with his women's backs. He could almost be said to have a fetish, in that to him, a woman's back seems to be the first thing he notices about her. A symbolist might also say that a woman's back is the last thing a man sees when she walks away from him. Perhaps Archer instinctively knows that these fleeting relationships with faceless beauties are impersonal, and that he will not [or cannot] make a lasting commitment to any woman, particularly one who is involved in one of his cases.)

In the last novel, however, newspaper woman Betty Jo Siddon seems to find a real place in his middle-aged heart, and she is the only woman who plays a larger role than a one-night stand. Significantly, she has played no part in the crime he is investigating, except as a fellow detective. She has all the qualities to win his heart—honesty, beauty, gentleness, intelligence, and a need for a man to build her self-image. When she disappears while digging for dangerous information for her news article, he becomes fearful and also begins to think in terms of love, something he admits he has not done in a long time. At the end of the novel he tells her a tale reminiscent of Moira's feeling like "Eve in the garden":

> There had been a time, it said, when men and women
> were closer than twins and shared the same mortal
> body. I told her that when the two of us came to-
> gether in my motel room, I felt that close to her. And
> when she dropped out of sight, I felt the loss of a part
> of myself.[25]

While Lew has discussed commitment with other serious romances, like Susanna Drew in *The Far Side of The Dollar*, Betty seems truly to have won Archer's heart. He is not a casual lover, and on the whole, his sexual relationships seem to be therapeutic rather than lustful or whimsical.

Archer's need for Betty at this stage of his life seems also to be related to the fact that he is growing older, and certainly he seems to grow lonelier as the novels progress. But Archer has always been preoccupied with aging, unlike most hard-boiled detectives who seem frozen—gun in hand—in time. In "The Bearded Lady" he recalls that although he and Western were close to the same age, he felt like the older brother. When Hendryx watches him outfight his ape-like body-guard, he tells Archer that he could have a future in fighting if he were younger.

In *The Moving Target* he has been married and divorced, reached thirty-five, and is aware that he is going to grow old and die. He notes that Graves, who is fortyish—not quite five years older than he—is wrinkled, balding, and developing jowls. In *The Drowning Pool*, he has been a detective for ten years, maintaining his quick, precise, youthful movements, but he has lost his enthusiasm. Mavis makes him wish he were younger, handsomer, and richer, and he describes himself as "a lonely cat, an aging tom ridden by obscure rage, looking for torn-ear trouble."[26]

"How did you get here?" in *The Way Some People Die*, receives the smart retort, "It all goes back about thirty-seven years ago."[27] Lt. Gary calls him "an aging boy wonder,"[28] and when he shows people Galley's picture, they inquire if she is his daughter—"the unkindest cut of all."[29] He is pushing forty in *The Barbarous Coast*, being called "old man," and describing himself as "middleaging."[30]

In *The Doomsters* he identifies with Ostervelt, seeing himself in such a bad light that he is forced to reprimand himself: "Self-pity is the last refuge of little minds and aging professional hardnoses."[31] Seventy-three no longer seems old to the detective rushing along to "premature middle age"[32] in *The Galton Case*, and Phoebe describes him, in *The Wycherly Woman*, as:

> a man in his early forties, quite good-looking in a raf-fish way, she says, with dark hair, blue-grey eyes; about six feet one or two, heavily built and muscular, with the air of an athlete. She took him at first for a professional athlete.[33]

In the later books there is considerable emphasis on the fact that Archer is "in very good trim, for a middle-aged man," and he accepts back-handed compliments like this with a grimace.

The carhop who brings him a hamburger calls him "dad." Conscious of being over forty in *The Zebra-Striped Hearse*, he tells Harriet Blackwell that he is old enough to be her father and Fawn King that he is too old for her and "getting older fast."[34] Arnie Walters accuses him of not seeing as well as he used to: "I hear senior citizens can get free glaucoma tests nowadays,"[35] and Archer graciously fails to retort that Arnie is older than he is. Although he refers to himself as "good old graying Lew Archer,"[36] he is not at all pleased with the suggestion that he retire and write his memoirs in *The Far Side of the Dollar*. Archer is approaching fifty in *Black Money*, and he compares

81

his age with that of his client's father. He panics when he has a vision of himself as "a middle-aging man lying alone in darkness while life fled by like traffic on the freeway."[37]

Recovering from a gunshot wound in *The Goodbye Look*, Archer confronts his mortality while resting in his easychair: "For just about the first time in my life I knew how it must feel to get old."[38] Looking in the mirror at the start of *The Underground Man* he notices "marks of erosion under my eyes, the mica glints of white and gray in my twenty four-hour beard."[39]

Again he is slightly annoyed that people think the girl whose picture he asks them to identify is his daughter. He is attracted to Jean Broadhurst but is held back by the reminder that he is almost twice her age. In *Sleeping Beauty* a cafeteria cashier wonders if he is Harold's father.

In *The Blue Hammer* Archer's relationship with a younger woman makes him all the more conscious of the older people in the case. Thirty years have passed since Richard Chantry's disappearance, and the main participants in his life are still around to be questioned. When they mention age, he good-naturedly points out, "I'm no spring chicken myself."[40] When the sheriff guarding Doris and Fred announces that he does not trust anyone under forty, Archer laments that he can really be trusted. The sheriff unnecessarily observes that he must be more like over fifty. The final blow is when Mildred Mead comments, "Isn't she a little young for you?"[41] when he admits he is interested in Betty.

Archer would be close to sixty in *The Blue Hammer*, and Macdonald lets him age naturally. There are fewer physical demands on the aging detective as he spends more time with domestic problems and crimes committed so long ago that the perpetrators themselves are broken and aging. Many of the criminals are women who force no showdowns or penitent men who regret their actions.

Archer uses more co-opted detectives instead of flying all over on a minute's notice or driving all night as he does in the early books. Macdonald lets him slow down, but hints that he stays in shape. Archer has given up smoking, has plain taste in food, drinks little, and has learned his limits.

In short, Archer is described as a real person with ordinary limitations, a mortal man among other dying people. He is like every man—only slightly more dedicated and ethical than most. He is a saint with everyday flaws that give him the humanity required of a priest in a secular world.

X.

SERMONS ON THE MOUNT

Life hangs together in one piece. Everything is connected with everything else. The problem is to find the connections.

—*The Far Side of the Dollar*

If there is one "priestly" quality in particular of which Archer can be accused, it is his tendency towards "preachiness." He often succumbs to the need to moralize at length, or at the very least, he cannot refrain from making a passing comment on moral issues relating to the case at hand. Actually, many of the novels can be read as "mini-sermons," and while Macdonald does not introduce extraneous material to support his own particular causes, he does allow his character to speak for him.

Many topics are grist for Archer's mill, but probably the broadest of his concerns relates to the individual's loss of the sense of "belonging" in modern society and to the concurrent demise of the family. Archer tends to speak in somewhat "homely" homilies:

> You can't blame money for what it does to people. The evil is in people, and money is the peg they hang it on. They go wild for money when they've lost their other values.[1]

> I learned that studying life. It's a course that goes on and on. You never graduate or get a diploma. The best you can do is put off the time when you flunk out.[2]

> Welfare begins at home.[3]

> The life you live may be your own.[4]

Many of these tidbits are simply overworked clichés voiced by someone who has spent a great deal of his time solving other people's problems. Archer admits he is a "moralist" in *The Moving Target*, apparently somewhat embarrassed by his overwhelming urge to philosophize. He has a sense of humor about it though, and obviously relishes his oneliners. In *Black Money* he says of four white-haired bridge players. "Three fates plus one, I thought, wishing there was someone I could say it to."5

Archer is often scolded for his proclivity for moralizing. Annoyed because he has evaded her questions, Helen Haggerty snaps: "You're full of copybook maxims....I want a serious answer."6 Bess Tappinger, angry because he will not fall into her arms, complains, "You're full of sententious remarks, aren't you? You're fuller than La Rochefoucauld, or my husband. But you can't solve actual problems with words."7 Mrs. Chantry growls: "Could you possibly spare me your generalization? I've been through quite a lot in the last twenty-four hours and I don't have the strength to listen to a cheap private detective mouthing moral maxims."8

Archer scolds his clients right back, particularly when they either refuse to accept responsibility for their actions, or, as they are wont to do, wallow in self-pity. He is capable of being cruel enough to shock people into action. He snaps at both the recently bereaved Kilpatrick in "Wild Goose Chase" and at Graves in *The Moving Target*, telling them in no uncertain terms what he thinks they should do to straighten out their lives.

Archer does not want to just solve crimes; he wants to resolve the conflicts that have created the climate for crime in the first place. He tells Rina in *The Barbarous Coast*: "You're a girl with a lot of conscience, and you've taken some hard blows. You have a tendency to blame yourself for things. You were probably brought up to blame yourself for everything."9 Similarly, in *The Way Some People Die* he tells Marjorie Barron that she made a mistake, but is not as stupid or worthless as she feels. On his advice she apologizes to her ex-husband, whom she had replaced with a drug dealer.

His frankness often forces people to become more involved when they would rather close their eyes to the situation. In *The Galton Case* Archer advises Roy Lemberg to stop putting his worthless brother before his lonely wife and reminds Dr. Howell that covering up for a patient violates his code of ethics. He implores the Crandalls to get psychiatric help for Susie in *The Underground Man*.

Not everyone, however, seems willing to listen to him. Alex Kincaid's father is too stubborn to admit that he needs to assume responsibility for Dolly, thus causing confusion for his weak son. Most of the time Archer's message is to support, not criticize each other. Only the courts, he seems to be saying, should attach blame.

Archer's coin of the realm is a strong dose of reality in a harsh and unforgiving world. He tells Jo Summers, for instance, that she deserved her rape and beating, (although he avenges her almost immediately after the tongue-lashing). He insists that people should face up to the problems that confront them, and act on them.

He is also a comforter, assuring Miranda that "Things never work out quite perfectly no matter how hard you push them."[10] He tells Alex Norris he is lucky to be alive, even though he has lost his girl and has been jailed for her murder. He urges the boy to stop feeling sorry for himself, and the boy snaps out of his depression so he can help find Lucy's real killer.

Archer's nemesis is the dope pusher, and he holds forth on the topic of addiction to Ruth, a heroin junkie who considers him "Mr. Drag" in *The Way Some People Die*:

> I've known weed and opium smokers, coke-sniffers, hemp chewers, laudanum drinkers, plain and fancy drunks, guys and girls who lived on canned heat and rubbing alcohol. There are even people in the world who would sell themselves into slavery for a long cool drink of ether. But your habit is the worst habit there is.[11]

Whether or not Ruth, who is bored by his lectures, will learn from his diatribe, Archer is determined to warn her about the serious consequences of drug use. The fact that he is mouthing platitudes does not make what he says any the less valid.

Perhaps the closest Archer gets to giving an honest-to-goodness sermon is when he advises Dolly not to give up praying because it keeps "the circuits open. Just in case there's ever anybody on the other end of the line."[12] This somewhat fatalistic observation is a rare reference indeed to religious faith in the novels.

He gives out a lot of practical advice, along with his philosophical maxims. He advises Burke Damis to write Anne Castle, whom he deserted for Harriet Blackwell. He advises Keith Sebastian to take Sandy to the psychiatric center instead of pretending that she is all right. He tells Stella, "Stay inside the safety ropes, with your own kind of people. You're much too young to step outside, and I don't think your parents are so bad. They're probably better than average."[13] He even gives advice on the care and feeding of junkyard dogs! "His teeth are dirty....You should give him bones to chew. I don't mean wristbones."[14]

Archer thoroughly dislikes men who prey on wealthy women, and, belying his hard-boiled heritage, he can be quite chivalrous. "As long as women own three-fourths of the property in this country, there will be men trying to take it away from them, and succeeding." He tells Kate Kerrigan that she belongs "to the biggest secret sorority in the United States....the ladies' auxiliary of the alimony fraternity."[15] And he compares a debutante ball to an African slave market.[16]

He also sympathizes with young girls who have fallen in love for the first time foolishly. The following comment on "California girls" is inspired by Sally Merriman, who is:

> one of those blondes who ripened early like California fruit, hung in full teen-age maturity for a few sweet months or years, then fall into the first highreaching hand. The memory of the sweet days stayed in them and fermented.[17]

Beautiful women, he notes have a hard time surviving; they become things rather than people (a surprisingly "modern" observation). Being treated as beautiful objects makes women see themselves as nothing but objects. An unattractive woman, on the other hand, uncomfortable with her lack of beauty, can become a dreadfully possessive wife.

Archer cagily attempts to avoid the extremes. "As a man gets older, if he knows what's good for him, the women he likes are getting older too. The trouble is," Archer observes, "that most of them are married."[18] The implied message is that a man who knows what is good for him will stay away from married women. And Archer, the inveterate advice-giver, will take his own.

Archer often works with extremely wealthy people, and social injustice is a familiar problem. Ralph Sampson in *The Moving Target* has long ignored the plight of his Mexican field hands, who endure low wages and terrible living conditions. To Archer, Sampson's refusal to allow his workers to strike for improvements will only lead to further mistreatment and manipulation.

And in *The Doomsters* Carl Hallman's dementia is seen as an outgrowth of the guilt he feels for his father's mistreatment of oriental orange pickers. Carl wants to turn the land over to the workers (an obvious sign of insanity to his wealthy family).

Archer admires the veritable promised land of the valley location of *The Wycherly Woman*. But he is also cognizant of the juxtaposition of swimming pool and air strip with the shacks and trailers of migrant workers. At the end of this tale, Phoebe, knowing that her father is a murderer, asks what will happen to him now. Archer replies cynically that rich men rarely see the inside of the gas chamber.

Archer also has some rather controversial ideas about bringing up children:

> Generation after generation had to start from scratch and learn the world over again. It changed so rapidly that children couldn't learn from their parents or parents from their children. The generations were like alien tribes isolated in time.[19]

One solution is to raise children anonymously thus preventing parents from living vicariously through their offspring, and allowing the children to live up (or down) to their own standards, not those set for them by their parents. He strongly recommends that parents allow children to make their own decisions and that they not expect their children to conform to their ideals.

On the other hand, Archer contends, somewhat equivocally, children who do not have good role models seem prone to turn to bad influences to fill the void. Parents *can* provide continuity and support, he seems to be saying, without forcing their children to be perfect little clones of their own ideals and behaviors.

Archer also voices another of Ross Macdonald's most obvious concerns, that of the protection of the environment. In *The Drowning Pool* Pareco oil company wants to buy Olivia Slocum's home and land for drilling purposes. Olivia becomes livid at the thought, and Archer learns that the community has banned such industry, seemingly in order to protect the environment: But ecological concern is only a euphenism for the landowners' real agenda—that of keeping out the Mexicans and dirty oil-crew workers who damage the town's prestige. Archer goes swimming, and while enjoying his freedom and solitude, muses that:

> They had jerrybuilt the beaches from San Diego to the Golden Gate, bulldozed super highways through the mountains, cut down a thousand years of redwood growth, and built an urban wilderness in the desert. They couldn't touch the ocean. They poured their sewage into it, but it couldn't be tainted.[20]

Archer is a full-blown nature-lover and he takes great joy in observing birds in their natural habitats. But it is not until *The Underground Man* and *Sleeping Beauty* that Macdonald's alter ego really begins to come to grips with the theme of encroaching ecological disaster and the social breakdown which often accompanies it. A major forest fire and a destructive oil spill dramatically symbolize the tainting of future innocent lives by crimes which have taken place in the past. The children in these morality tales must surely pay the price of their fathers' sins. Corrupted family pasts are darkly silhouetted against the backdrop of present-day ecological disaster, and Archer is forced to come to terms with his own nightmarish vision of the future.

In *The Underground Man* Archer actually experiences a "nightmare" at the beach wherein he sees future populations swelling to cover every square foot of the Earth. A loner by choice, he finds this vision abhorrent, and imagines a stratum of smoke covering the city so that "The low sun was like a spinning yellow frisbee which I could almost reach out and catch."[22] The sunbathers and swimmers seem oblivious to the conflagration around them.

While discussing the troubled Susie and the kidnapped Ronny, Joy Rawlins and Archer have an interesting side conversation about the Dunes Bay pelicans whose bodies are so poisoned with DDT that their eggs are too fragile to hatch. Society, it seems, gives no more thought to the destruction of its bird young than it does to its human children.

These pelicans will continue to haunt Archer as a symbol of what happens when men and women put short-term pleasures before legitimate future concerns. He worries particularly about Jerry Kilpatrick, then fatalistically concludes: "He had to live out his time of trouble, as she (his mother, Ellen) had. And there was no assurance that he would. He belonged to a generation whose elders had been poisoned, like the pelicans, with a kind of moral DDT that damaged the lives of their young."[22]

In *The Wycherly Woman* Helen Trevor tells Archer that her husband puts Phoebe ahead of her or his own welfare: "He's been fixated on my brother's child ever since she was born."[23] Trevor insists that parents do not kill their own children, and Archer tells him to read the papers. Parents *are* capable of ruining their children's lives, and dysfunction in families *can* motivate murders.

When Archer becomes aware of Alice and Gordon Sable's troubled relationship, it provides the key to unlocking past and recent crimes.

These neglected young are capable of striking out against their elders and society, as we see in *Sleeping Beauty*. Archer, flying in from Mazatlan, views the huge oil spill from above: "An offshore oil platform stood up out of its windward end like the metal handle of a dagger that had stabbed the world and made it spill black blood."[24] With this ugly vision a story begins to unravel of an ancient crime that has blighted the lives of three children and causes much pain and suffering for their families.

Archer meets the beautiful Laurel Russo by chance, as both mourn a western grebe so covered with oil that Archer does not recognize it immediately. He describes the bird's orange-red eyes as "burning with anger."[25] He subsequently becomes involved with Harold Sherry, a young man who is also burning with anger. Labeling himself as someone who is concerned with the environment, Archer rules out Captain Somerville's theory that an environmentalist must be seeking revenge. He wishes that "we could live like the birds and move through nature without hurting it or ourselves."[26]

At the conclusion of the book, Archer learns the true story of the oil spill on Canaan Sound. He forges a link between the oil spills, a thirty-year-old murder, and two recent killings. Laurel's grief is not only over the grebe's death, but she must mourn for her mother's crime as well.

By refusing to acknowledge the truth, these families have suffered pain and misery, which continues to fester over the years, like poison in a wound. Archer and Somerville end by staring at "the unreality expanding between us until it lay like a pollution over the endless city and across the endless sea, all the way to Okinawa and the war."[27] Archer's job as always, is to make all the connections vital to a case. But, as he is well aware, the most common cause of murder will be found hidden within the failure of the family unit. Since domestic violence is so redundant in his work, Archer remains vitally concerned about it, and the novels continue to sermonize against the breakup of families.

From the first story, "Find the Woman," to the last novel, *The Blue Hammer*, Archer operates as a "missing persons" specialist. Admitting that he is primarily a divorce detective in his civil work, Archer spends most of his criminal investigation time either looking for lost family members or dealing with people who, because of problems in the family, have become criminals or potential criminals.

Significantly, eight of the novels begin with Archer's being hired to find a family member who has disappeared: a husband in *The Moving Target*; a daughter in *The Way Some People Die*; a housekeeper (a surrogate family member) in *The Ivory Grin*; a grandson in *The Galton Case*; another daughter in *The Wycherly Woman*; a wife in *The Chill*; another son in *The Far Side of the Dollar*; and still yet another daughter in *The Instant Enemy*. These cases usually begin as searches for apparent runaways, and, inevitably, more missing people turn up during the investigation.

The Underground Man is a search for a kidnapped child, Ronny Broadhurst. Archer becomes involved because he and the boy live in the same apartment house and have had a good relationship. As usual, the case becomes more complex as it unravels. In *Sleeping Beauty* Archer is attracted by Laurel Russo, whose grief over a dead bird does not seem enough of a motive for suicide. Archer undertakes a desperate search to find her before she overdoses on sleeping pills, and in the process, uncovers a series of interconnecting losses and murders. Interestingly, he feels morally obligated to find Ronny and Laurel, even though initially he has not been hired to do so.

The Zebra-Striped Hearse and *Black Money* both begin with requests to investigate suspicious men wanting to marry rich girls. Mark Blackwell hopes to protect Harriet from a gold-digging artist, Burke Damis, and Peter Jamieson wants the handsome, mysterious Francis Martel exposed so he can get his girl back. In both novels the couples disappear and Archer's search for them uncovers murder.

Even what appear to be simple cases can turn into complicated affairs. *The Barbarous Coast* seems at the outset to involve just another routine detective job. Bassett, the manager of "The Channel Club," hires Archer on as a bodyguard to protect him from the infuriated George Wall, who believes Bassett is involved with his wife, Hester. But Archer begins to sympathize with Wall, and the bodyguard job shifts to a search for the missing Hester, a task which is increasingly complicated by the uncovering of other crimes.

In *The Goodbye Look*, the Chalmers hire Archer to find a simple missing box, a seemingly uncomplicated task, but by the third chapter their son turns up missing too, and Archer is drawn into a search for several lost people.

A painting has vanished from the Biemeyer mansion in *The Blue Hammer*, but before he finds it Archer locates a missing husband and son!

Find A Victim finds Archer stopping to assist a man who has been fatally shot. He becomes involved in the search for a missing girl, whose personality is described so vividly by her lover, her father, and her sister that Lew, when he finds her body, is blinded by tears.

Archer is hired to find Reavis and bring him back in *The Drowning Pool*, but the real story involves the reuniting of a father and daughter when their family is in danger of disintegrating through violence.

The same type of family failure occurs in *The Doomsters*. Carl Hallman has come to Archer, ostensibly for help, but then he knocks out the detective and steals his car! Carl seems to be a homicidal, vengeful maniac, but, in reality, he is a missing brother, and after his death, the story of past crimes unfolds to explain why his family fell apart.

Archer himself is a "loner." He has lost his wife through divorce, and his memories of his own family imply that they are all deceased. Because of his background he is strongly motivated to preserve the integrity of the family unit.

Disintegration of the family, in fact, is a common thread in these novels, a deterioration reflected by (and perhaps a result of) the concurrent breakdown in society which allows crime to flourish unchecked. The people Archer deals with in his cases have very often lost someone dear to them, either literally or metaphorically. These are "lost" people themselves who have deliberately hidden their identities and created a whole world of lies. (Ross Macdonald has admitted to being drawn to the theme of the lost father since he himself was abandoned by his own father at an early age.)

The Underground Man, *Sleeping Beauty*, *The Blue Hammer*, *The Chill*, *The Barbarous Coast*, *The Zebra-Striped Hearse*, *The Ivory Grin*, *The Doomsters*, *The Instant Enemy*, and *The Galton Case* all deal with past crimes that have affected numerous lives, led to disintegration of families, and necessitated further violence. Over the years Macdonald has veered away from the ubiquitous Las Vegas mobsters and their ilk and moved toward crimes committed by ordinary people driven by remorse, revenge, or guilt to kill.

"The Suicide" actually describes two suicides. Clare Larrabee says her father has "passed away," leaving the sisters extremely dependent upon one another. Without their parents' support, the girls have used whatever means they can to get by. Mrs. Falk, however, tells Archer that, after the girls' mother left, the father drank himself into a depression and shot himself.

In "Wild Goose Chase" a little girl pathetically asks Archer if he is her daddy. Not long after, her mother is killed, leaving her truly an orphan, and a representative of all of society's children who so desperately want to belong but are merely shunted from place to place.

Hester Campbell, in *The Barbarous Coast*, lied to her husband, intimating that she was an orphan. In reality though, she had a sister, Rina, and a mother who "was bound to make something out of those girls if it killed them."[28] Their father had been a well-known silent movie actor, and before age and an unnaturally high voice precluded his working in the talkies, the family had lived in a huge Beverly Hills mansion. Hester gets back the family home through blackmail, and dies there.

Another character, Isobel Graff, is psychotic, jealous and dangerous after years of drug and alcohol abuse. She is still mourning her father, who had called her "Princess." His death had triggered a series of breakdowns:

> I thought I was in the coffin. I felt dead, my flesh was cold. There was embalming fluid in my veins, and I could smell myself. At the same time I was lying dead in the coffin and sitting in the pew in the Orthodox Church, mourning for my own death. And when they buried him, I could hear the earth dropping on the coffin and then it smothered me and I was the earth.[29]

Isobel blames herself for wishing her mother dead and for breaking her father's heart. Carrying a load of guilt deepened by her husband's affairs and Bassett's manuevering of her, she is driven into madness and becomes one of the saddest depictions of the "fatherless child" in the Archer novels.

The most dangerous of these waifs is Galley Lawrence in *The Way Some People Die*. She is a mass murderer, and seems, if anything, even more vicious than the gangsters she moves among. She tells Archer that his snoring reminds her of her father, whom she loved and lost when she was eight. Another lost girl in this novel is Ruth, who remembers walking along the beach with her father and their cocker spaniel. These happy childhood memories contrast vividly with the pain of the loss she experienced when both parents deserted her. Lest Archer criticize her father, however, she hastens to add that he sends money and writes letters. Her grandmother has no influence over the unhappy girl, whose boyfriend leads her easily into a life of drug abuse and crime.

In fact Macdonald's tales are full of a whole series of young men and women whose lives have been ruined through the loss of a father. In *Find A Victim* Jo Summers' father dies in an accident: "They gave him a draft exemption because he worked in the shipyards, and then they went ahead and killed him anyway."30 But even before his death he had gone off with another woman. Jo's mother and her new boyfriend let Jo run wild instead of going to school, and, badly confused, she ends up marrying a crook.

Mildred Hallman's father ran away when she was young and left her with an alcoholic mother who grumbles: "Mooning all the time over her no-good father. You'd think *she* was the one that married him."31

In *The Zebra-Striped Hearse* the drunken Mrs. Buzzell declares that she can no longer keep track of her son, Ray, one of the youngsters in the hearse. But Ray seems to be a basically good kid in spite of his lack of parenting.

Unfortunately, Ray seems to be the exception. Most of Archer's "fatherless children" are in much worse shape. Artist Burke Damis is angry, immature, and self-centered. He tells Archer that his father, a Chicago policeman was: "A bad act. I remember the last time I saw him. I was eighteen at the time, hacking my way through art school. He was helping a blonde into a Cadillac in front of an apartment door on the Gold Coast."32

Kitty in *Black Money* was basically a good girl until her father became ill and spent two years in the County Hospital with little or no real medical care. Kitty has become "hard as nails," and she blames her mother for the situation. Typically, Mrs. Sekjar cannot understand why beating Kitty bloody did not straighten her out!

In *The Far Side of the Dollar* Ralph Hillman rejects his adopted son, Tommy, who prefers music to sports. Ralph instead acts as a surrogate father for Dick Leandro, who works on Ralph's boat (and who was deserted by his own father as a child). Tommy, as a result, feels compelled to search for his real dad. The dénouement, however, reveals that Tommy *is* Hillman's real son, and not adopted after all. Tommy's boarding school chum, Fred, tells Archer that many of the children there believe that they must be adopted, since their families show so little interest in them. "He said he couldn't know who he was until he knew for sure who his father is." (Wistfully he adds that he wishes Archer were his father.)33

During this investigation Archer also becomes acquainted with Susanna Drew, whose father, a professor at UCLA, has been supervising her studies. Although he is dead now, he still seems to control her life. Susanna tells Archer about the archetypes (Oedipus, Hamlet, and Stephen Dedalus) her father taught in his courses. This theme of fatherless children parallels the somewhat desperate search Tommy is conducting for his own "lost" father.

In *The Goodbye Look* Jean Trask is passionately convinced that her father, who had run off with another woman long ago, is still alive. She and her husband, George have a heated discussion over her obsession, which reminds Archer of the words and deeds that drove his own wife, Sue, away. Jean's father ran away when she was sixteen, and at thirty-nine she is still unwilling (or unable) to give up on her search. Oblivious to her present situation, she declares:

> I'm going to find my Daddy....I'll find him dead or
> alive. If he's alive I'll cook and keep house for him,
> And I'll be happier than I ever was in my born days.
> If he's dead I'll find his grave and do you know what
> I'll do then? I'll crawl in with him and go to sleep.[34]

In *The Underground Man* Archer and others search for Ronny, Susan, and Jerry, all children who have lost their fathers. Stanley Broadhurst is obsessed with the fact that his father, Leo, has run off with another woman, leaving the twelve-year-old brooding about the desertion for the next fifteen years. Now he is gradually cracking mentally, and spends more time on his search than with his family or his job. Like Jean, he dies because his search is successful. Stanley is killed and (ironically) thrown into his missing father's grave.

Stanley is not the first generation of his family to suffer, however. His mother, Elizabeth, has the same ambivalent feelings for her own father. Although he had lost the family's holdings and spent most of his time puttering about as an amateur ornithologist, to Elizabeth he was a great man. In her memoirs she writes about his killing of songbirds "for science" (one of her hobbies is killing birds with her father's target pistol), calling it a painless bestowal of the gift of death. Her handwriting deteriorates as she concludes in a defensive scrawl that: "Robert Driscoll Falconer, Jr., was a god come down to earth in human guise."[35]

Elizabeth is a "daddy's girl," rich, attractive, and totally unemotional, and Leo Broadhurst had good reason to leave home. *The Underground Man* is based on the distintegration of the family through fixations centered on the image of the lost father, and the lack of will to work on new relationships. In reality, people should not need to conduct such desperate searches for their fathers in order to demonstrate their grief.

Among the fatherless children are several, including Ethel Larrabee, Galley Lawrence, Isobel Graff, and Mildred Hallman, who, unfortunately, have resorted to murder to assuage their feelings of anger and despair. Others perform criminal or at the very least anti-social acts that are associated with the murders Archer is investigating. Some are driven into destructive behavior when their parents threaten to disown them if they don't conform.

As we also have seen, the vacuum left by an absent father is very often filled by a domineering mother. Thus Olivia Slocum makes James feel ineffectual, and Mrs. Snow actually directs the murder charges on to her son, Fritz.

Lost mothers are not so frequent, but they are equally likely to cause problems. Alice Turner loses her mother (in "The Bearded Lady,"), and her father turns to an unfaithful young woman who ends up seducing Alice's fiancé! The Larrabee girls' mother causes their father's death. Reginald Harlan blames their mother's divorcing their father for his sister's unfortunate choice of a husband. Miranda Sampson dislikes her stepmother intensely. Tony in *The Barbarous Coast* explains the difficulty of raising his murdered daughter Gabrielle by saying that she lacked a mother's guidance. Hilda and Meyer together cannot replace the mother who died in giving birth to Anne, so she runs wild and dies as a result. When Peter Jamieson's mother dies, his psychological problems are made manifest by his compulsive eating habits. The death of Allie Russo in *The Sleeping Beauty* casts a blight, not only on her son, Tom, but also on his wife Laurel, as well as Harold.

Thus Archer's world is full of the victims of the loss or misguidance of one or both parents, and he remains sensitive to the effects such deprivation can have on people. And Archer is well aware of an individual's need to uncover the clues to his present identity by coming to grips with the secrets of the past.

Interestingly, there are far more examples of Archer's mercy and understanding of the criminals he confronts than there are of his condemnation of them. Archer, who seems consistently cognizant of his own personal losses, has an uncanny ability to empathize with those who seem compelled to express their grief and loneliness by striking out against society.

Furthermore, through his role as "detector," Lew Archer has evolved a method by which he can effect a positive influence on society, while others (like Davy Spanner of *The Instant Enemy* or Carl Hallman of *The Doomsters*) fail utterly, and are even killed for acts for which they are not responsible.

When she first hires Archer, Mrs. Galton insists that Anthony Galton must be alive somewhere because: "Nothing is lost in the universe." "Except human beings," Archer thinks to himself.36 And indeed this statement could be called "Archer's Maxim." Only people can be lost, and many of them, in Archer's world, are. Can such devastating losses be prevented? Archer obviously believes that it is the family unit which lies at the root of man's salvation, and it is no coincidence that Macdonald repeatedly places his detective right square in the midst of family squabbles in order to demonstrate how failure to communicate, or lack of communication altogether, can cause havoc by destroying such relationships.

Husbands and wives are in frequent conflict. A fight between Dr. Sylvester and his drunken wife, Ella, gives Archer a great deal of information in *Black Money*. Langston's commitment to his ex-student, Davy Spanner, is so strong in *The Instant Enemy*, that he leaves his worried pregnant wife to undertake the search with Archer.

A clue is unearthed during a fight scene in *The Blue Hammer* when Jack and Ruth Biemeyer toss out accusations at each other on the subject of Mildred Mead. Jack retorts that if Ruth had given him sex he would not have run after her. Archer grasps the full implications of that argument much later.

These fights seem to occur just when people need each other the most, and they often result in painful exchanges and attempts to cast blame. *The Far Side of the Dollar* is one of several novels in which family quarrels precipitate crimes.

Archer contacts the families involved in order to get at the roots of a boy's disappearance. The Harleys are a child abuser and his broken wife, who has knowingly allowed him to beat the two young boys and treat them like animals.

Robert Brown and his wife blame each other for their daughter Carol's ruined life. Mrs. Brown has entered Carol in beauty contests, inundating her with false hopes and dreams. Mr. Brown (who has made a surrogate son of Mike Harley) is accused of rejecting his own daughter while he works at being an adored coach and counselor. Caught in the middle of these mutual accusations and recriminations, Archer recommends that the couple pull together or risk destroying each other. He intervenes even more directly in this family's problems than he usually does, and even suggests that they see their minister for counseling.

The third dysfunctional family in this tale, the Hillmans, are torn apart by grievances which have been allowed to fester through the years. Blackmail and murder are among the woes which have come to dominate their lives. Ralph Hillman has rejected his so-called "adopted" son Tommy, and has accepted Don Leandro as a surrogate son. Carol and Susanna have displaced his wife Elaine long ago. Instead of fighting openly, the Hillmans continue to hide their conflicts behind a façade of lies.

Not until Archer finds Tommy and brings him back home are they able to confront each other openly. Through these people's stubborn refusal to communicate with each other, four people die unnecessarily. Tommy is a basically good boy, and supported by his sensible friend, Stella, he will hopefully be able to lead a normal life. Archer always has hope for the children.

The children suffer once more, in *Sleeping Beauty*. There is the same familiar pattern of lack of openness, in this novel, that hints of unsatisfactory relationships and the shutting out of a part of the family.

Archer visits the Lennox family, expressing his urgency at finding Laurel before the pills she took can be fatal. Lennox, on the other hand, seems preoccupied with the oil spill, and both parents radiate disapproval of their son-in-law and his cousin-housekeeper, Gloria. Their chief concern seems to be for the possible loss of their father's estate to his second wife! Lennox, in fact, slaps his wife, sending her into dry-eyed tears and disconcerting Archer, who observes laconically: "They were one of those couples who couldn't pull together."37 Lennox warns Archer to be "discreet" about the incident.

He next visits the Somervilles, where he finds that Captain Somerville is closer to his ex-steward, Smith, than he is to his wife, Elizabeth. When she reproaches Smith for taking pot-shots at rats inside a building, Somerville snarls at her that he "gives the orders."

If the Archer books are any indication, the modern family is in a lot of trouble. Broken homes are common, as are: children confronting stepparents; brothers and sisters who engage in criminal activities together; demanding mothers-in-law; fathers who commit incest (or other kinds of abuse); couples who mask inner conflicts with an outer rosy façade; all these scenarios and more are among the familial conflicts which are grist for Macdonald's literary mill. His world view, in fact, seems to be telling us that the family unit, rather than providing a stable and loving environment, more often than not precipitates the disorder and violence which are the natural milieu of his genre.

In each of these novels, however, Archer speaks out against such conflicts within the family. And while he disapproves of the deeds, he takes care never to characterize the people who commit them as evil. These are tormented souls, driven by misery and despair, and they usually succeed only in making their situations worse. Their problems are often rooted in the past, where some sort of false relationship or situation has created a fabric of lies that inevitably shreds, leaving the child with nothing to hold on to.

Archer intervenes in these affairs and forces his clients to face up to reality. Unfortunately, however, he is usually called in years after the initial damage has been done, and can only make a belated attempt to rescue the children. In case after case, Archer tries to establish moral stasis first, and restore what is salvageable within the family unit, before he calls in the police. He functions like an Old Testament prophet crying out in the new urban wilderness. Case closed and sermon ended.

XI.

THE TIE THAT BINDS

Willie was no saint, but he was an honest man according to his lights, even if the lights were neon.
—The Wycherly Woman

The hard-boiled detective needs no Watson to test his theories or to demonstrate his brilliance. He prefers to solve his problems alone and he narrates his own stories. Archer, however, does not walk completely alone down California's mean streets. He has a number of people to whom he turns regularly, and they can also be seen to serve as a kind of surrogate family unit as well. Several people appear regularly in the Archer stories, but Peter Colton, Willie Mackey, Arnie and Phyllis Walters, Morris Cramm, and Glen Scott would seem to be his closest professional allies.

Archer worked under Peter Colton in Army Intelligence during World War II. Peter is Archer's "main man" in the District Attorney's office who gives him advice and information when he most needs them. He first appears in *The Moving Target* as a senior investigator.

Colton does not welcome Archer with open arms immediately, although the detective settles in comfortably anyway. He describes Peter and his surroundings succinctly as: "a heavy middle-aged man with cropped fair hair and a violent nose like the prow of a speedboat inverted. His office was a plaster cubicle with a single steelframed window." Their conversation is banter, "a vaudeville act."[1]

Colton knows Archer is there for free information and does not want to spend too much time away from his stack of police reports to provide it. The suggestion is formed that this is a familiar pattern for their encounters. They work together for their mutual benefit (although Colton accuses Archer of using his office for basic legwork he is too lazy to do for himself), and Colton agrees to help.

In *The Barbarous Coast* Colton has recently retired (although Macdonald later puts him back to work). He is a good source of information about organized and unorganized crime, and is willing to provide Archer with the background he needs. Colton has been frustrated in the past by the difficulties involved in prosecuting known Syndicate members, especially when the police are their bodyguards and the politicians are their fishing companions. Thus it soon becomes clear that Peter Colton is not only willing to share his facts with Archer, he shares his idealism as well.

In *The Zebra-Striped Hearse* Colton tells Mark Blackwell that Archer operates the best one-man agency in Los Angeles County. In *The Far Side of the Dollar* Archer mentions that he has "bullyragged my friend Colton, the D.A.'s investigator, into asking Sacramento for Harold or Mike Harley's record, if any."[2] Colton has become an important link between Archer and the law, and his name arises frequently whenever Archer is brought into a police station for questioning and needs a reference.

In *Find A Victim* Archer lists three kinds of people who end up in the courthouse: the amiable failed lawyer; the rising politician; and "the public servant who would rather live in a clean community than please a friend or get his picture in the paper."[3] Colton is just such a dedicated public servant, and the private detective obviously respects and admires him, much as he respected and admired his Uncle Jake during his youth.

Willie Mackey is Archer's San Francisco alter ego. He is first mentioned in *The Wycherly Woman* when Homer Wycherly hires Archer to investigate the letters that accused his wife Catherine of having an affair. Saying only that they had worked together several times, Archer describes him thus:

> Willie was a flat-faced man in his late forties with black eyes that had never been surprised. He wore a narrow black moustach, a white carnation in the buttonhole of his Brooks Brothers suit; and managed to look a little like a headwaiter. Women adored him, if you could believe his personal decameron. I liked him pretty well myself.[4]

The two detectives have similar likings for Gibsons and steaks. Both are aware of the aging process, both are shrewd judges of character, and both are angry when a case is blocked by bureaucrats. Unlike Archer, however, Willie maintains a large, highly-successful practice. His office suite contains four or five rooms, complete with Persian carpet, mahogany furniture, a couch, filing cabinets, and a glass showcase for his trophies. Willie owns a Jaguar, in contrast to Archer's old Ford convertible, and his ornate office has been redecorated with red upholstery.

Willie gives Archer all the Wycherly documents, summarizes the case for him, and promises to watch for information, even though he is too busy to help much.

In *The Instant Enemy* Archer calls Willie for help and Willie agrees (although he resents having his sleep disturbed). Still, he assembles the information Archer needs quickly and meets him at the San Francisco Airport:

> I found Willie in the airport bar drinking a Gibson. He was a smart experienced man who copied his style of life from the flamboyant San Francisco lawyers who often employed him. Willie spent his money on women and clothes, and always looked a little over-dressed, as he did now. His gray hair had once been black. His very sharp black eyes hadn't changed in the twenty years I'd known him.[5]

In *The Underground Man* Archer calls Mackey at his apartment, on the top floor of his office building, and a girl answers. He suggests that Willie call him back later, which he does, explaining to Archer that he has gotten married again.

Willie is familiar with the Broadhurst case, primarily because of the large reward which has been offered, and he sets about to find Ellen Kilpatrick for Lew. Archer learns that Ellen is using the name of "Storm," and Willie Mackey working fast, with a large staff of operatives and informants, has her house staked out by the time Archer arrives in San Francisco. Jerry Kilpatrick is captured by Willie and his large assistant, Harold (who takes care of the physical end of things). Archer is able to talk Susie out of committing suicide, and Willie uses his influence to keep the local police from arresting the girl. Like Archer, Willie gets along well with children, and he soon has Ronny sleeping on his lap.

Willie, who shares a brotherly conviviality with Archer, is, perhaps, the detective Lew might have been, had he taken a slightly different direction. In spite of their contrasting mode of operation, they make a good team.

Arnie and Phyllis Walters are Archer's Nevada "connection." They operate an agency in Reno that blankets that end of the state. Phyllis is once referred to as an ex-policewoman, and another time as an ex-Pinkerton operative. She combines an official-sounding voice with feminine exuberance, but to Archer's eye she resembles an ex-chorus girl.

Arnie is in his early fifties and looks "like somebody you'd see selling tips at a race track."[6] Archer describes Arnie as "a Reno colleague of mine who had split more than one pint with me."[7] The three of them get along well together, and they all share the attributes of a good detective—honesty, imagination, and curiosity. The Walters are efficient, fast in their work, and, most importantly, they, like Archer, care about people.

Since Archer works night and day when he's on a case, he pulls the Walters out of bed more than once. Phyllis answers his phone call in *The Chill*, saying she hasn't seen him in so long that she wonders if he is just a voice on tape that someone plays for her now and then.

At Archer's request, Phyllis contacts and befriends Sally Burke, a possible witness for him. When she meets him at the airport, her normally peaches-and-cream complexion strikes Archer as being a little the worse for wear, and she admits that she has to work at staying beautiful these days. (She has gotten drunk with Sally the night before, in order to hold her for Lew.)

Archer gets his information from Sally and ends up in a fist fight with her brother. He is taken to the police station, but Arnie follows him in to make sure he's not booked, then drives him to the Bradshaws' and patiently plays cards while Archer talks to the couple. Archer notes that "One of the things that made [Arnie] a first-rate detective was his ability to merge with almost any group, nest into almost any situation, and start a conversation rolling" (Archer could just as easily have been talking about himself).8

Lew spends the night in the Walters' guest room, then has breakfast with them before returning to Los Angeles. A cozy picture of fellow detectives operating as a family unit begins to emerge. Arnie and Phyllis do things for Lew that go way beyond professional assistance. They really are his friends. What may be even more significant, in Archer's eyes, is the fact that this couple has stayed intact. Not only do they respect each other as working partners, there is evidence that they respect each other as marital partners as well. Archer and Mackey have never been able to achieve such a conjugal relationship, have remained "loners." Arnie and Phyllis may function then, as spiritual "parents" to Lew, reassuring him that, in a troubled world, the concept of "family" is still a viable and valid goal.

The fourth "good" detective appears only briefly, in *The Doomsters*, but he can be presumed to be a long-time colleague. Glen Scott is a retired Los Angeles detective, and the "old master" of the group. Archer is acquainted with Scott's wife, Belle, and he asks about their children. He loses a game of chess to Scott, who then kids Archer about his "crusades," declaring that the only things in life worth having are a place to call home, a wife, family, and enough money to be comfortable. He comes to Archer's aid in this case, but he also seems to serve as a kind of "father confessor" to the younger man. Even a dean of detectives must retire eventually, he seems to be suggesting, and serve only as a consultant.

It is hard to imagine Archer retired and at ease, like Scott, from the world he has known and loved in spite of its horrors. Neither is he just a businessman like Willie Mackey or a part of an efficient team like Arnie and Phyllis.

Archer is a new breed of detective, a crusader for new solutions to old problems, and unlike his hard-boiled brethren, he continues to maintain his good relations with the police. His initial encounter with Captain Royal in *The Wycherly Woman*, however, is hostile. The Redwood City police consider Archer a material witness, or even a suspect, but he is definitely not a favorite of theirs. Even Peter Colton's name cannot work its magic here.

Carl Trevor, however, is rich and powerful, and Archer considers him a good colleague, though somewhat inflexible. In *The Zebra-Striped Hearse*, Trevor endures the uncooperative Damis' insults patiently, while questioning him. His attitude toward the man most people have assumed to be a killer is that: "I think he's a bum. I also think he's got a fair shake coming to him,"9 and Archer agrees completely with the big policeman.

In *The Galton Case* Archer meets Deputy Mungan, a big, craggy, powerful man who impresses him immediately by his sharpness and thorough training. Like Archer he has a past, a short experience with illegal liquor and women. Now Mungan is a policeman, dedicated to controlling organized crime. He is another crusader, and in this case Archer can quite honestly announce that he is working with the police.

In *Black Money* Archer is impressed with young Ward Rasmussen, who is concerned with people, has ambitions to be a detective, and is willing to work on his own time. Over breakfast, they share information about Martel. Archer sees himself as he had been twenty years earlier when he talks with Rasmussen.

Another policeman, Captain Perlberg, is a respected acquaintance with "a kind of enveloping Jewish force."10 Perlberg calls on Archer to talk to Martel's Panamanian mother, trusting him to avoid an international incident. (Such trust between the police and Phillip Marlowe, for instance, would have been unlikely.)

In *The Far Side of the Dollar*, the detective is knocked out by some unknown party and rousted by the police, who even take away his wallet. A fuming Archer is rescued by Lieutenant Bastian, one of the best policemen he will meet in his career, and, accordingly, cooperates with him more fully than he does in most cases. Bastian provides him with money for phone calls and even arranges a per diem and travel allowance for him since he is between clients. "Bastian was a saturnine Puritan, absolutely honest, a stickler for detail, a policeman before he was a man,"11 Archer thinks, watching the lieutenant stand up to an arrogant Hillman.

Other helpful and likeable policemen Archer comes in contact with are: Merceno, a CHP dispatcher, who provides license plate IDs in *The Galton Case*; Detective Sergeant Sam Garlick, a tailor's son who is an expert at identifying clothing, and who traces a suit in *The Zebra-Striped Hearse*; and Roy Snyder of the Bureau of Criminal Investigation in Sacramento, who checks the ownership of a gun in *The Goodbye Look*. Their expertise and willingness is invaluable to Archer.

In *The Instant Enemy* he admires detective sergeant Prince, who, like Archer, was a Golden Gloves boxer who could have gone bad but chose police work instead.

Lew is also impressed by Captain Aubrey, who takes an interest in Sandy Sebastian, since he has a daughter her age and is aware that young people can be pushed over the line between good and evil easily. Archer appreciates Captain of Detectives Arnie Shipstad and Joe Kelsey of the Forest Service for their precise minds for detail and for their determination in separate but related investigations in *The Underground Man*. Considering the positive experiences Archer has with the police, it is not surprising that he identifies with them, and that he has such enormous respect for authority.

Outside his fellow detectives and other lawmen, Archer has a wide range of acquaintances who provide him with valuable information. Lawyers Bert Graves and Gordon Sable turn out to be criminals, but young, inexperienced, and honest Jerry Marks proves a valuable ally. Movie people—like writer Sammy Swift, agent Joey Sylvester, and script writer Russell Hunt—are frequent sources of information. Joshua Severn and Susanna Drew are friends who are television producers.

Morris Cramm appears in *The Moving Target* and *The Drowning Pool* to provide his encyclopedic knowledge gathered as a night legman for a newspaper columnist in Los Angeles. Manny Meyer is an art critic; Coney, a bellhop at the hotel where Archer stays when he is in San Francisco. People in all types of work are equally useful to a detective.

The fellows with whom he went surfing as a young man do not appear in Archer's life any more. His private life is mentioned only in brief allusions to his youth, casual parties, and neighbors. Judging from the way he works with others, however, Archer has chosen his solitude in order to allow him to do his work more effectively—a self-imposed "priesthood."

Archer is at his best when dealing with those who need help. His best friends seem to be in the ranks of those who have a similar mission in life. Although he enjoys their company, he calls on them only when he needs their cooperation. As Sue complained, justly perhaps, Archer has a tendency to give way too much of himself—and it interferes with the time he has to spare for personal relations.

In spite of his being without a family or any kinds of relatives, Archer genuinely likes children, and they reciprocate his affection. In "Wild Goose Chase" he meets seven-and-a-half-year-old Janie, a beautiful, quiet girl who wonders if he is her daddy. The child goes through the ordeal of finding her mother dead, and Archer gently questions her, takes her by the hand, and asks the cabdriver to tell her a cheerful story while he calls the sheriff's office and her father. Even during a murder investigation, he considers the well-being and security of the child more important than reporting the crime. In *The Galton Case* he travels to Redwood City to talk to Mrs. Matheson about the missing Galton family. Finding her eleven-year-old son James home alone, practicing his push-ups, Archer watches the boy and chats with him about his Little League coach, and Archer's high school football days. Before long the two are tossing a football back and forth, until the angry mother arrives and spoils the mood. But even when Marion Matheson bursts into tears, James does not blame Archer for his mother's upset.

In *The Far Side of the Dollar* Archer is hired to find a boy, Tommy Hillman, who is missing from the Laguna Perdita School for troubled teenagers. Everything about the school has the feel of a prison. To Archer the boys move

> like members of a defeated army. They reminded me
> of the very young soldiers we captured on the Rhine
> in the last stages of the last war."[12]

One of the boys, Fred, comes up and nudges Archer, almost like a dog testing for friendliness—and asks him if he is a father. When Archer treats him like an intelligent adult, the lad responds by providing him with new information. As he talks, Archer senses his desolation and damaged self-concept. He also observes that the youths react negatively to the supervisor, who addresses them in a dehumanizing manner. Archer empathizes with the young men, and later Fred gives Archer one of his most treasured compliments by telling him that he wishes Lew were his father.

The detective befriends Tommy Hillman's friend, Stella Carlson whose parents have forbidden her to see or talk to the boy. Though her parents treat her like a wayward child, Stella will not allow her parents to disparage Tommy. She follows Archer in order to tell her side of the story, and they become colleagues in the search for Tommy. He explains what he is doing and she provides certain insights that lead him to the real problem which has brought about the boy's disappearance.

When Mrs. Carlson charges into the woods to confront Archer and Stella talking about Tommy, Archer assures her that no harm will come to her daughter so long as he is around and that she is a decent young woman now, and no longer should be treated as a child. Archer is upset that Rhea and Stella have been driven apart by the case, and he works hard trying to get the Carlsons back together all the while he is searching for the Hillman's son.

He respects Stella's intelligence, and sympathizes with her as "one of those youngsters who make you feel like apologizing for the world."[13] She runs away from home and talks the manager of his apartment house into letting her in, but he whisks her away to Susanna

Drew to provide her with a "proper" chaperone. Stella is a normal, forthright girl. Archer tries to convince her that not all adults are bad and that her parents truly care about her. But he eventually realizes she will have to discover these things for herself.

Archer and Stella develop a genuine father-and-daughter relationship, sometimes serious and sometimes light-hearted. He tells her that "Happiness comes in fits and snatches" and she asks him frankly about his relationship with Susanna Drew. Like a good detective's daughter, Stella provides a great deal of information to Lew by observation and by eavesdropping when Hillman visits Susanna.

Typically, Archer will look after a child during the time parents are so deeply involved with a problem that they cannot provide proper understanding and support, but he refuses to come between them. Eventually he sends Stella back home, reassuring her that in his opinion her parents are better than most.

The relationships Archer develops with Fred and Stella are warm, and are no different from those he has with adults. There are no secrets or evasions between them, whereas their personal problems, and even the crimes the detective has been hired to solve, are the result of the lies of their elders.

When John Truttwell hires Archer to find the Chalmers' lost gold box in *The Goodbye Look*, he expresses dislike for their son, Nick, who is engaged to his daughter, Betty, "the nicest thing I'd come across in some time."14 Nick Chalmers turns up missing, and Archer and Betty quickly develop a good relationship, strengthened in part by Archer's pleasure at discovering that the girl is a good "finder-outer" who can assist him not only through her concern for her fiancé, but with her intelligence as well.

Betty's father, after losing his wife, has become very possessive of his daughter. She knows that many of the problems between her father and she are because he had lost his wife when she was younger than her twenty-five-year-old daughter is now. Accustomed to being treated like a child, Betty appreciates Archer's attitude. He treats her as an intelligent human being.

Betty is aware of Archer's tendency to "adopt" people and causes. He tells her, quite honestly, without elaborating, that "I've done a lot of counseling in an amateur sort of way," and she chides him for trying to cheer her up by advising her to go home and read a good book.

As she cleans the lipstick from his face. she asks about his affair with Moira. Betty turns the tables on Archer, treating him as she would her own father if he were involved in something of which she did not approve.

In *The Blue Hammer* he is especially concerned with Doris Biemeyer and Fred Johnson, whose lives have been torn apart by their parents' conflicts and lies. When he finds the two, he talks to each of

them, giving them confidence and assurance that things will straighten
out for them.

Archer serves as defender for and protector of the young, and
he suffers for those who are victims just as much as he does for those
who have been murdered. Archer most regrets the dilemma of little
Martha in *The Doomsters*, the only innocent and unspoiled person in
the Hallman family: "It wasn't fair that her milk teeth should be set on
edge."[15] The sins of the father, Archer's experience corroborates, are
visited on the children like Martha.

Archer easily takes on the role of father for people of all ages.
In *The Name Is Archer* he recalls protecting his military partner, Hugh
Western, who seemed oblivious to danger. After the artist's murder,
Archer takes care of his sister, Mary, even advising her not to work so
hard.

He often protects young women in his cases, which creates an
ambivalence of sorts between his fatherly concern and his more lustful
sexual feelings. Seeing pretty Clare Larrabee on the train, Archer befriends her, aware that she is too young and innocent for him. But he is
delighted to be seen with a woman who turns all eyes as she walks by.
(As the story unfolds, however, Archer learns that she and her sister are
unscrupulous and desperate.)

Hester Campbell's sister Rina, a nice girl, assumes that she
should thank Archer by going to bed with him. In the early part of
The Moving Target Miranda Sampson makes a pass at Archer just to
make Alan Taggert jealous. When her act fails to move either man, she
and Archer develop a good relationship that allows for openness between them.

In reality many of the women Archer has befriended either
cause or commit crimes, and there is a disproportionate number of
women murderers in these novels. His relations with such criminally
inclined women—Galley Lawrence, Ruth, the drug addict, Kitty
Ketchel, Bess Benning, Jo Summer—never quite get off the ground,
although he always sympathizes with them, and even promises Mrs.
Lawrence that he will testify in Galley's defense.

The women with whom he has the best relations are the
daughters of families who have both over-protected and underestima-
teed them. These are good young women for the most part, who have
become involved with troubled or unscrupulous men. They are willing
to form a relationship with Archer based on their recognition that he is
trying to help them. In these cases he assumes a role of father-protector
of sorts, and promptly begins to lecture them, as he does with Sheila
Howell in *The Galton Case*:

> Give yourself some thought too....I know it doesn't
> seem likely, but if he is an imposter, you could be
> letting yourself in for a lot of pain and trouble.[16]

105

When she cries, he feels guilty, conscious that others might disapprove of men who make pretty girls cry. But her father, Dr. Howell, handles her far less successfully when he orders John Galton to leave the Country Club at once and finds that Sheila is no longer under his control.

Archer is in touch with the times, and although he's a bit preachy, he could never be accused of being autocratic. In a time of crisis he knows young people need the respect, concern, and understanding of someone who can help them examine their options rather than demand unquestioning obedience. At the end of *The Galton Case* Sheila marries Galton, who turns out to be the genuine heir, as she has instinctively known all along. Archer's faith in her judgment has been justified.

In *The Underground Man* Archer takes Jean Broadhurst under his wing, aware all the while that she is an attractive young woman. After he talks Susan Crandall out of suicide, Archer questions her gently, eliciting from her the memories of the past that explain two murders and the deep disturbance that has made her so hard to control. He takes her mother aside and suggests that she share her own past with Susan to show that she is human after all.

These relationships with substitute daughters, no matter how meaningful, are temporary. Not only do they not carry from one novel to the next, they are not really part of the conclusions to the mystery (with the exception of *The Galton Case*). The closest thing to a "carryover" to another book is Miranda Sampson's recommendation of him in *The Way Some People Die*. It appears that once he completes a case he never sees his "daughters" again.

The same is true for the surrogate sons in Archer's life. Pat Reavis is one for whom Archer serves as "keeper." Although Archer dislikes him, his grief is intense following the young man's death, and is directly traceable to the fact that he had lost someone whom he was trying to guard.

Archer becomes the volunteer keeper for a number of young men who are not criminals. George Wall desperately needs a keeper in *The Barbarous Coast* because "He had a fine instinct, even better than mine, for pushing his face in at the wrong door and getting it bloodied."[17] Both shed a lot of blood over a woman who is not worthy of her idealistic though bumbling husband. As soon as Wall sees Archer, he trusts the detective to get a message through to the intended victim. Archer cares for him until the case becomes more complicated. Then Archer leaves Wall behind.

Peter Jamieson in *Black Money* has lost the love of his life, Ginny Fablon, to a richer, more handsome, and more mysterious man. Archer prefers Ward Rasmussen, the young patrolman who is extremely helpful to him. But Ward is too stable to need his concern. Peter manages to stay out of harm's way while he eats his way through the case.

He and his father have a very weak relationship, and Mr. Jamieson drinks with the same compulsive intensity as his son eats.

Archer's descriptions of the young man's eating habits are at once comic and pathetic. Just before Marietta Fablon is killed, Peter devours most of a cold roast goose. When he tells Archer that he is still hungry, Peter's voice is "fogged with grease."[18] Archer advises him to see a psychiatrist, warning him that Ginny will be appalled at those grotesque eating binges. He considers his relationship with Peter unique: "I think in my nighttime loneliness I'd fathered an imaginary son, a poor fat foolish son who ate his sorrow instead of drinking it."[19]

In *The Chill* Alex Kincaid needs help getting his bride of a few days back. A wise son, Kincaid can handle every situation except dealing with his domineering father. Overcoming his past diffidence, however, he helps Archer clear Dolly of murder charges in spite of his father's insistence that he drop both the wife—and the detective. Archer admits to a secret pleasure that Alex turns to him rather than to his father: "I felt vaguely gratified. I was old enough to be his father, with no son of my own, and that may have had something to do with my feeling."[20] After Dolly explains about her mother's murder under Pentothal, she and Alex are out of the case.

Fred Johnson of *The Blue Hammer* begins as a suspect and ends as a surrogate son. In this case the parents are so unpleasant that Archer has no difficulty in sympathizing with the boy. He discovers that Fred is actually trying to help Doris Biemeyer and to learn the truth about the "Chantry" painting, and Archer suspects that the two of them have a lot in common.

When the young man breaks down and cries bitterly in their motel room, Archer comforts him with the fact that without a previous record he will not be condemned easily. He assures Fred that he still has a future. At the same time, Archer is gathering evidence—such as the fact that the paint is not only new, but the style is an obvious development of Chantry's. He also learns that the boy had not seen his father before he was seven-years-old and that his mother's bad treatment of his father seems to him to be revenge for ruining her life. This "foolish pseudo-son"[21] has given him information that will help him solve the case.

There are several other "pseudo-sons" for whom the detective develops feelings. Among them is Ronny Broadhurst, whose kidnapping Archer investigates in *The Underground Man*, and Alex Norris, whom he talks out of despair and proves innocent of murder. He gets personally involved with these young men. At the same time he is solving his cases, he is also handing them advice on straightening out their lives. His obvious concern goes way beyond his professional involvement and, within the context of our discussion here, could be seen as falling under "priestly duties." Lew Archer is an invaluable advisor to the youths he meets along the way.

The troubled young people whom he accepts as surrogate sons and daughters fill his life only so long as the cases in which they are involved remain open. Aside from the memory of his ex-wife, Archer has no lasting intimate relationships, although he is willing to listen to other people's confessions without betraying them, giving even criminals understanding and support. He understands people in the manner of a dedicated confessor.

XII.

CONCLUSION: FATHER CONFESSOR

This man knows about me, too, I can see it in his face.

—*The Galton Case*

In the above quote,[1] the tormented Alice Sable has identified one of Archer's most unique traits, as well as one of his priestly characteristics: he invites confession. His own honesty and concern for others, in fact, make it difficult to lie to him, or to hold anything back.

Sometimes Lew has cause to regret this ability to inspire confidence. Nevertheless, Archer listens to secrets, not only at the dénouement of his cases, but all along the way. He characteristically responds to these confessions with remarks like: "It's safe with me," "My lips are sealed," and "I'm a clam." Clients and criminals alike seem to know they can trust Archer with their secrets.

His first, rather jocular, comment about his role as confessor is made as he refuses to get in Terry Neville's car: "I listen better standing up. I always stand up at concerts and confessions."[2]

Mrs. Dreen confesses her love for her son-in-law and her method of arranging Una's death. Archer confronts her with her guilt, but does not turn her in to the authorities. In "Gone Girl" Mr. Salanda, the girl's father, tells Archer all about his irrational desire for big, dumb blondes. At the end of "Wild Goose Chase," Glen Cave tells Archer, who has no way to prosecute the crime, exactly how he maneuvered Rhea Harvey into murdering for him.

In these stories, Archer is omniscient when someone is lying, though he does not accuse anyone directly. Sooner or later he will find the truth, just as sooner or later the Caves will be punished.

In *The Barbarous Coast* Archer senses that the desk clerk is about to tell Archer about her divorce problems. "I braced myself for another life-story. Something about my face, maybe a gullible look, invited them."[3]

Many different people open up to him. In *The Drowning Pool* Olivia Slocum shares with Archer her innermost feelings toward the valley and her hatred of the oil company that is trying to make her sell it. She senses that Archer understands and sympathizes with her.

Mavis Kilbourne, a woman of another type, tells him of her brief romance with Pat Reavis, her miserable life with her wealthy husband, her blackmail pictures, the porno film, and her terrible taste in men. Gretchen Keck, a very young hooker, answers all of Archer's questions trustingly. Knowing how troubled they are, he finds resisting their charms quite simple. A very different woman, the competent professional, Mildred Fleming, relates all of Maude Slocum's past and thanks Archer for listening, though they have never seen each other before.

Some confidences come from unlikely sources. Though he has been at odds with Archer throughout *Find A Victim*, Sheriff Brand Church confesses: his involvement with Hilda; his inability to deal with his mentally-ill wife, and his realization that she never loved him; his need to be needed; his grief at not having children; and, his losing battle with his desire for Anne! After listening to all this, Archer can understand why Church has covered up so much of the crime.

Homer Wycherly, in spite of his oil revenues, takes quickly to Archer, revealing not only his fear of driving, but also his problems with his wife, soon after they meet. Later, Carl Trevor tells Archer about *his* unhappy marriage and the turbulent long-lived affair he has been having with his sister-in-law.

In *The Zebra-Striped Hearse* Mark Blackwell's compulsion to confess actually drives his daughter to commit murder. He makes a long, dishonest statement which gives a false solution to the case. Blackwell's "need to tell" is a form of masochism.

His wife, Isobel, finally provides the needed information about her first husband's death. For a long time she has withheld her connection to Dolly Campion's murder, but at last she spills out her frustrations, as Archer observes, "justifying her life and its meanings."[4] When she wonders why she recites these things from her past, Archer explains that chloral hydrate has some truth serum properties. But his presence has helped inspire her.

After hearing the stories from Mark and Isobel, Archer goes to Mexico to confront Harriet about the murders. She says that she has already tried to tell the priest there, but her Spanish was not good enough. "But you're no priest," she protests, when Archer offers to listen to her instead.[5] He reassures her that although he is just a layman, she can feel free to tell him everything, including her motives—and she does, agreeing at the same time to return with him to face up to her crimes.

Her final, and surprisingly simple, confession resembles the explanation of the crimes to which Mildred Hallman was driven in *The Doomsters*—or Marian Lennox's last conversation with Archer in *Sleeping Beauty*.

Archer learns that Marian had kept her crime a secret until Harold Sherry began wreaking revenge on the family. All three of these women are least-likely-suspects who might have gone free if they had been able to lie to the persistent, but caring detective.

In *The Galton Case* Archer learns a good many secrets. Marian Culligan Matheson tells him about her ill-fated first marriage to a gambler whom she hoped to reform, saying, "I don't know why I'm telling you all this. I've never told a living soul in my life. Why don't you stop me?"[6]

He listens because he needs all the information he can get and he *is* patient. Another woman with serious family problems, Mrs. Lemberg, tells Archer about her husband and his dishonest younger brother. She too wonders why. "I don't know why I'm telling you all this. In my experience, the guys do most of the talking. I guess you have a talk-at-able face."[7]

While Archer is hospitalized in Reno, Sable remonstrates, "You're a willing man, but you can't take on responsibility for all the trouble in the world."[8] Sable himself confesses at the end of the investigation, expressing relief that the whole thing is over. Archer feels sorry for him, as he does for John Galton's mother with her sordid past.

In *Black Money* Dr. Sylvester's drunken wife tells Archer about the Fablon family's history and her husband's involvement with it. After a while she becomes anxious about what she has said. "I've been telling you my deep dark secrets, haven't I?", she announces, embarrassed that she has shown so much malice.[9] Another lonely wife, Bess Tappinger, tells Archer a great deal about herself, including her attempt to lure Martel away from Ginny at a party. Then she stops. "I think Taps brought you here to have me confess. My husband is a very subtle punisher."[10]

Although Archer establishes his greatest rapport with women, Harry Hendricks also informs Archer of his past as a hopeless loser. Archer learns that he lost his wife Kitty to Leo Spillman (or Ketchel), in a crap game! Archer's kindness in getting him to a hospital and offering to pay for good medical attention allows Hendricks to share his past so freely. When Harry says, "I'm the biggest failure west of the Mississippi. I don't even deserve to live," Archer responds in his best fatherly manner, "Everybody deserves that."[11]

In *The Far Side of the Dollar* Archer hears more confessions than he wants to. Mrs. Mallow, the housemother at Laguna Perdita, talks about herself as well as the boys. She tells Archer that after dealing with adolescents all the time, she finds it difficult to function in the outside world. "People around here are extraordinarily ready to spill their problems," notes Archer.[12]

Archer complains that her discussions with him don't have anything to do with his case. Her concern for her young charges wins his admiration, however, and she senses his approval enough to let him know she's free on Saturday nights.

Susanna Drew, though she is an old friend, does not respond immediately to his invitation to tell him her troubles—"Another time, doctor,"[13] she answers hesitantly, unsure if he is speaking as her friend or as the detective probing for facts. Later on she admits her involvement with Tommy's mother, Carol Harley, and Ralph Hillman. When Archer accuses her of being paranoid, she again responds sarcastically: "Yes, Doctor. Shall I stretch out on this convenient couch and tell you a dream?"[14]

Archer and she begin to work out Tommy's troubled past. Archer is firmly convinced that all things are connected, and he truly believes that it is possible to make seemingly diverse facts fit together if people will only talk them out objectively.

The Hillmans have been in denial about the ugly past, and Elaine Hillman concedes her resentment against her husband and his past unfaithfulness. She tells Archer that, except for Ralph, she has never told anyone else, preferring instead to suffer in silence. Her New England stoicism has driven her to violence. Archer's advice: "It might be a good idea to ventilate it,"[15] comes too late. When Elaine asks how he can possibly know so much about other people's lives, he answers that his business is people, the only things he can see in the world. His ability to concentrate on them as individuals inspires both confidence in him—and confession to him.

The misunderstandings that have led to Tommy's confusion and several deaths gradually emerge, based in part on the confessions these two women are willing to make to Archer. Like Susanna, people are always ready to spill their whole life's story, just as soon as Archer sits down with them to listen.

In *The Goodbye Look* Betty Truttwell marvels: "I've spilled all my secrets. How do you make people do it?"[16] Archer, taking no credit for skill or personality, says simply: "I don't. People like to talk about what's hurting them. It takes the edge off the pain sometimes."

Bernice Sebastian becomes angry with Archer for conducting his "catechism" in *The Instant Enemy*, particularly when he asks about Sandy's sexual experience. When she insists that sex has nothing to do with the matter, he counters, "People are always telling me that about their central concerns."[17] Archer will not accept either a false or a partial confession. He will dig patiently for every piece of the puzzle, whether his subject confesses freely or not.

In *The Underground Man* Mrs. Snow tells Archer about Broadhurst's affair with Ellen Kilpatrick, and then blushingly adds, "I don't know why I'm telling you all this. I intended to go to my grave without telling anyone."[18]

Joy Rawlins shares a great deal of her past and her feelings toward Susan Crandall and her whole family, knowing all the while that she is talking too much. She is also aware that Archer is pumping her for information. She answers anyway because she cares for Susan and senses that he does too. After she is fired, Joy angrily tells him about Martha Crandall's past.

Whatever the motive for the confession, however, the information that is given not only helps Archer identify the killer, but it makes it possible for him to understand the motive behind the killing as well. Several of the confessions are made by the killers themselves. Often these come before Archer has come up with a complete solution to the mystery. In these novels the detective listens humbly and sympathetically.

Hidden facts emerge slowly in *The Blue Hammer*. Several secrets, in fact, are thirty years old. Archer recognizes that there is something that the Biemeyers have long been afraid of dealing with: "I was an unwilling referee who let them speak out on their old trouble without the danger that it would lead to some thing more immediate, like violence."[19]

This passage may explain why Archer is so often caught up in the middle of domestic squabbles. He allows people to confess rather than keep resentment pent up inside until they can't help but explode in violent and unacceptable ways.

Doris Biemeyer tells Archer about her parents' continual arguing and their lack of love for each other. These miserable memories of family life have led her to take drugs. When Archer advises her that downers cannot help her straighten up her life, she pouts, "Nobody asked you for your advice. You are a shrink, aren't you?...I can smell the dirt on you, from other people's dirty secrets."[20] Doris cunningly perceives that Archer invites confessions by his very nature. Ruth Biemeyer finally tells Lew about her past when she learns how much he knows about Doris' feelings. She also admits that she is checking her lawyer for divorce procedures, noting, "I shouldn't be telling you all these things."[21]

Usually Archer comes in contact with people who are concerned that he not think ill of them. He cannot hide his initial shock at the statements Jake Whitmore's girl makes about the man with whom she lived, and she hurriedly explains that she only wants to sell the paintings in order to get his body out of the county hospital for a decent coffin and burial.

Sometimes he and his witness "confess" to each other. Archer's admission that his grandmother wanted him to be a priest occurs while he is talking with Paula Grimes, who is mourning her father's death. He has told her that he is not a cop, but "runs a small business." The fact that they are speaking in the chapel makes his half-truth seem shameful to him, and he must control his own urge to confess the truth to Paula. She reveals much about her father, including the sordid fact of his passion for young boys and his hope of discovering a "new" Chantry.

Confessions such as these, as we have seen, help Archer find solutions to his cases. But many of his clients sense that Archer is a rather peculiar detective whose aims have a deeper purpose than merely catching thieves and putting them away in prison.

He has evolved from his early police training, when he saw everything in terms of good-and-evil. He now understands that people make judgments about the right thing to do at a particular juncture in time, and that often these judgments are based on emotion. He does not condemn anyone out of hand when he or she makes a mistake. He has come to know that the pain and suffering of criminal and victim alike is all part of the human condition.

Henri J. M. Nouwen has defined the proper attitude of anyone involved in the priesthood as that of a "contemplative critic."

> He does not bounce up and down with the fashion of the moment, because he is in contact with what is basic, central, and ultimate. He does not allow anybody to worship idols, and he constantly invites his fellow man to ask real, often painful and upsetting questions, to look behind the surface of smooth behavior, and to take away all the obstacles that prevent him from getting to the heart of the matter. The contemplative critic takes away the illusory mask of the manipulative world and has the courage to show what the true situation is. He knows that he is considered by many as a fool, a madman, a danger to society, and a threat to mankind. But he is not afraid to die, since his vision makes him transcend the difference between life and death and makes him free to do what has to be done here and now, notwithstanding the risks involved.[22]

Archer's style of detection would seem to agree with Nouwen's description of a "contemplative critic." He enters the crime as an equal participant in the suffering of victim and criminal alike. Having once been in trouble himself, though briefly, he has the ability to empathize with the criminal, who may have taken the wrong path. He does not look down upon those with whom he comes in contact, either mentally or morally.

Archer is, in Macdonald's words:

> a man who is in touch with the ordinary and content to be fairly ordinary. And at the same time he has moral interests and humane interests which are reflected not so much in what he does, but in how he does it. He takes his job seriously. I mean he's not just concerned with running down a criminal. He's

concerned with the whole interrelationship of people that produces crime and is affected by crime. His primary interest is in understanding other people's lives. And trying to make sense of them.[23]

Archer's distinctiveness as a detective, then, is that as he solves the crime, he also takes the time to discuss the motivations *behind* the crime. He does not dwell on his cleverness at catching crooks. His unique use of confession allows the criminal to talk through whatever he or she has done. When all the loose ends are tied up and the innocents are exonerated, life returns to normal. When the crimes are solved, it is as if they had never been. The case has ended and moral harmony has returned to the family or social unit. People may start their lives over, free from past blame and guilt. Thus Archer the detective has fulfilled many of the obligations and duties of a humanist priest within the framework of a secular society.

NOTES

Chapter I

[1]Raymond Chandler, in *The Simple Art of Murder*, p. 20-21.
[2]An essay by Robert B. Parker which appeared in the entry on Raymond Chandler in *Twentieth-Century Crime and Mystery Writers, Second Edition*, ed. John M. Reilly. NY: St. Martin's Press, 1985, p. 153.

Chapter II

[1]Sam Grogg, Jr. "Ross Macdonald: At the Edge," in *The Journal of Popular Culture* 7 (Summer, 1973): 221-222.
[2]Henri J. Nouwen. in *The Wounded Healer*, p. 41.

Chapter III

[1]"The Bearded Lady," p. 74.
[2]*Ibid.*, p. 75.
[3]*Ibid.*, p. 111.
[4]*The Moving Target*, p. 2.
[5]*Ibid.*, p. 137.
[6]*The Galton Case*, p. 11.
[7]*The Wycherly Woman*, p. 3.
[8]*The Underground Man*, p. 189.
[9]*Ibid.*, p. 180.
[10]*The Zebra-Striped Hearse*, p. 12.
[11]*Ibid.*, p. 63.
[12]*The Blue Hammer*, p. 5.
[13]*Ibid.*, p. 169.
[14]*Ibid.*, p. 14.
[15]*Ibid.*
[16]*Ibid.*, p. 40.
[17]*Ibid.*, p. 99.
[18]*Ibid.*, p. 249.
[19]*Ibid.*, p. 269.
[20]*The Moving Target*, p. 53.
[21]*The Drowning Pool*, p. 71.
[22]*The Far Side of the Dollar*, p. 39-40.
[23]*Black Money*, p. 462.
[24]*The Name Is Archer*, p. 9, *The Wycherly Woman*, p. 175, *The Moving Target*, p. 70, 50, 182, *The Underground Man*, p. 181, *Black Money*, p. 37.
[25]*The Way Some People Die*, p. 124.
[26]*The Wycherly Woman*, p. 115.

Chapter IV

[1]*The Blue Hammer*, p. 197.
[2]"Find the Woman," p. 17.
[3]"Gone Girl," p. 43.
[4]"The Bearded Lady," p. 100.
[5]*The Moving Target*, p. 101.
[6]*Ibid.*, p. 6.
[7]*The Drowning Pool*, p. 139.
[8]*The Way Some People Die*, p. 184.
[9]*Ibid.*, p. 114-115
[10]*Find A Victim*, p. 165.

11 *The Barbarous Coast*, p. 401.
12 *The Doomsters*, p. 237.
13 *Ibid.*, p. 250.
14 *Ibid.*
15 *The Instant Enemy*, p. 30.
16 *Sleeping Beauty*, p. 74.
17 *The Blue Hammer*, p. 19-20.
18 "The Bearded Lady," p. 76.
19 *The Drowning Pool*, p. 200.
20 *The Way Some People Die*, p. 25.
21 *Find A Victim*, p. 151.
22 *The Wycherly Woman*, p. 37.
23 *Sleeping Beauty*, p. 206
24 *Black Money*, p. 426.
25 *The Far Side of the Dollar*, p. 99-100.
26 *The Instant Enemy*, p. 7.
27 *Sleeping Beauty*, p. 86.
28 *The Ivory Grin*, p. 3.
29 *Ibid.*, p. 68.
30 "The Bearded Lady," p. 99.
31 *The Moving Target*, p. 121
32 *The Drowning Pool*, p. 179.
33 *Ibid.*, p. 208.
34 *The Way Some People Die*, p. 30.
35 *The Barbarous Coast*, p. 416.
36 *Ibid.*, p. 520.
37 *The Moving Target*, p. 63.
38 *The Drowning Pool*, p. 11.
39 "Gone Girl," p. 55.
40 *The Barbarous Coast*, p. 483.
41 *The Ivory Grin*, p. 20.
42 *The Moving Target*, p. 82.
43 *The Chill*, p. 283.
44 "The Suicide," p. 158.
45 *The Moving Target*, p. 35.
46 *The Barbarous Coast*, p. 508.
47 *The Drowning Pool*, p. 202.

Chapter V

1 *Find A Victim*, p. 112.
2 *Sleeping Beauty*, p. 158.
3 "The Bearded Lady," p. 88.
4 *The Barbarous Coast*, p. 472.
5 *The Wycherly Woman*, p. 18.
6 *The Blue Hammer*, p. 123.
7 *The Instant Enemy*, p. 132.
8 *The Goodbye Look*, p. 11.
9 *The Far Side of the Dollar*, p. 159.
10 *The Goodbye Look*, p. 25.
11 *The Galton Case*, p. 150.
12 *The Goodbye Look*, p. 96.
13 *Ibid.*, p. 178.
14 *The Blue Hammer*, p. 164.
15 *The Underground Man*, p. 76.

Chapter VI

1 *The Moving Target*, p. 125-126.
2 *The Drowning Pool*, p. 94.
3 *Ibid.*, p. 184.
4 *Ibid.*, p. 213.
5 *The Wycherly Woman*, p. 99.
6 *The Drowning Pool*, p. 26.
7 *The Instant Enemy*, p. 200.

[8]*Sleeping Beauty*, p. 100.
[9]*Ibid.*
[10]*The Zebra-Striped Hearse*, p. 52.
[11]*Find a Victim*, p. 158.
[12]Sam Grogg, Jr. "Ross Macdonald: At the Edge," in *Journal of Popular Culture* 7 (Summer, 1973): 217-218.
[13]*The Zebra-Striped Hearse*, p. 1.
[14]*Ibid.*, p. 10.
[15]*The Drowning Pool*, p. 2.
[16]*The Barbarous Coast*, p. 45.
[17]*The Wycherly Woman*, p. 65.
[18]*Ibid.*, p. 53.
[19]*The Zebra-Striped Hearse*, p. 147.
[20]*The Drowning Pool*, p. 141.
[21]*The Way Some People Die*, p. 172.
[22]*The Ivory Grin*, p. 140.
[23]*The Chill*, p. 412.
[24]*Black Money*, p. 595.
[25]*Ibid.*, p. 218. Jean Cocteau (1889-1963) was a French author, artist, and film director.
[26]*The Ivory Grin*, p. 65.
[27]*The Zebra-Striped Hearse*, p.107.
[28]*The Chill*, p. 208.
[29]*The Far Side of the Dollar*, p. 25.
[30]*Ibid.*, p. 86.
[31]*The Underground Man*, p. 13, 139.
[32]*Ibid.*, p. 162.
[33]*Sleeping Beauty*, p. 65.
[34]*The Zebra-Striped Hearse*, p. 52.
[35]"Find the Woman," p. 5.
[36]*Ibid.*, p. 1, 3.
[37]*The Moving Target*, p. 103.
[38]*Ibid.*, p. 98.
[39]*The Zebra-Striped Hearse*, p. 1.
[40]*The Galton Case*, p. 40.
[41]*Sleeping Beauty*, p. 194.
[42]*The Drowning Pool*, p. 3.
[43]*The Barbarous Coast*, p. 412.
[44]*The Way Some People Die*, p. 113.
[45]*The Galton Case*, p. 126.
[46]*The Zebra-Striped Hearse*, p. 10.
[47]*The Galton Case*, p. 132.
[48]*Ibid.*, p. 180.

Chapter VII

[1]*The Name Is Archer*, p. 113.
[2]"The Suicide," p. 157.
[3]*Ibid.*, p. 159.
[4]*The Way Some People Die*, p. 173.
[5]*The Ivory Grin*, p. 232.
[6]*The Blue Hammer*, p. 266.
[7]*The Moving Target*, p. 169.
[8]*Black Money*, p. 454.
[9]*The Moving Target*, p. 176.
[10]"The Bearded Lady," p. 67.
[11]*The Blue Hammer*, p. 151.
[12]*The Name Is Archer*, p. 99.
[13]*The Far Side of the Dollar*, p. 159.
[14]*The Moving Target*, p. 176.
[15]*The Barbarous Coast*, p.499.
[16]*The Way Some People Die*, p. 99.
[17]*Ibid.*, p. 101-102.
[18]*Ibid.*, p. 130.
[19]*The Moving Target*, p. 82.

[20] *Ibid.*
[21] *Ibid.*, p. 184.
[22] *Black Money*, p. 588.
[23] *Sleeping Beauty*, p. 45.
[24] *The Far Side of the Dollar*, p. 118.
[25] *The Moving Target*, p. 4.
[26] *The Barbarous Coast*, p. 442.
[27] *The Doomsters*, p. 69.
[28] *The Name Is Archer*, p. 236.
[29] *The Wycherly Woman*, p. 64.

Chapter VIII

[1] *Sleeping Beauty*, p. 92.
[2] *The Blue Hammer*, p. 120.
[3] *Ibid.*, p. 126.
[4] *The Moving Target*, p. 40.
[5] *Ibid.*, p. 41.
[6] *Ibid.*, p. 3.
[7] *The Drowning Pool*, p. 77.
[8] *The Galton Case*, p. 108.
[9] *The Wycherly Woman*, p. 106.
[10] *The Zebra-Striped Hearse*, p. 138.
[11] *The Instant Enemy*, p.115.
[12] *Ibid.*, p. 527.
[13] *The Name Is Archer*, p. 74-75.
[14] *The Barbarous Coast*, p. 442.
[15] *The Way Some People Die*, p. 102.
[16] *The Far Side of the Dollar*, p. 38.
[17] *The Instant Enemy*, p. 76.
[18] *The Far Side of the Dollar*, p. 206.
[19] *The Barbarous Coast*, p. 493.
[20] *The Galton Case*, p. 387; See also: *The Wycherly Woman*, p. 107.
[21] *Sleeping Beauty*, p. 72-73.
[22] *The Galton Case*, p. 31.
[23] "Gone Girl," p. 39.
[24] *The Drowning Pool*, p. 174, 183.
[25] *The Barbarous Coast*, p. 398.
[26] *The Chill*, p. 286.
[27] *The Drowning Pool*, p. 113.
[28] *The Doomsters*, p. 238.
[29] *Ibid.*, p. 250.
[30] William Ruehlmann, in *Saint With a Gun: The Unlawful American Private Eye*, p. 105.
[31] *The Drowning Pool*, p. 26.
[32] *The Doomsters*, p. 151.
[33] *The Drowning Pool*, p. 46.
[34] *The Goodbye Look*, p. 149.
[35] *The Chill*, p. 278.
[36] *Black Money*, p. 514.
[37] *The Blue Hammer*, p. 60.

Chapter IX

[1] *Find a Victim*, p. 111.
[2] *The Moving Target*, p. 13.
[3] *The Way Some People Die*, p. 112.
[4] *The Barbarous Coast*, p. 394.
[5] *The Doomsters*, p. 174.
[6] *Ibid.*, p. 251.
[7] *The Zebra-Striped Hearse*, p.108.
[8] *The Goodbye Look*, p. 96.
[9] *The Underground Man*, p. 181.
[10] *Sleeping Beauty*, p. 67.
[11] *The Blue Hammer*, p. 99.

[12]*The Way Some People Die*, p. 6.
[13]*The Galton Case*, p. 153.
[14]*The Wycherly Woman*, p. 271.
[15]*Ibid.*, p. 96.
[16]*Black Money*, p. 491.
[17]*Ibid.*, p. 535.
[18]*Ibid.*, p. 540.
[19]*Ibid.*, p. 580.
[20]*The Instant Enemy*, p. 131.
[21]*The Goodbye Look*, p. 114.
[22]*Ibid.*, p. 115.
[23]*Sleeping Beauty*, p. 68.
[24]*Ibid.*, p. 198.
[25]*The Blue Hammer*, p. 250.
[26]*The Drowning Pool*, p. 81.
[27]*The Way Some People Die*, p. 65.
[28]*Ibid.*, p. 116.
[29]*Ibid.*, p. 31.
[30]*The Barbarous Coast*, p. 387, 389.
[31]*The Doomsters*, p. 123.
[32]*The Galton Case*, p. 21, 183.
[33]*The Wycherly Woman*, p. 247.
[34]*The Zebra-Striped Hearse*, p. 20, 120.
[35]*The Chill*, p. 258.
[36]*The Far Side of the Dollar*, p. 186.
[37]*Black Money*, p. 601.
[38]*The Goodbye Look*, p. 151.
[39]*The Underground Man*, p. 6.
[40]*The Blue Hammer*, p. 87.
[41]*Ibid.*, p. 220.

Chapter X

[1]*The Moving Target*, p. 182.
[2]*The Wycherly Woman*, p. 241.
[3]*The Chill*, p. 275.
[4]*Black Money*, p. 622.
[5]*Ibid.*, p. 444.
[6]*The Chill*, p. 229.
[7]*Black Money*, p. 539. François, Duc de La Rochefoucauld (1613-1680) was a French writer known for his *Maxims* (1665), "a collection of more than 500 moral reflections and epigrams, generally paradoxical, often pessimistic, and usually acute"— *The New American Desk Encyclopedia*.
[8]*The Blue Hammer*, p. 205.
[9]*The Barbarous Coast*, p. 506.
[10]*The Moving Target*, p. 74.
[11]*The Way Some People Die*, p. 147.
[12]*The Wycherly Woman*, p. 211.
[13]*The Far Side of the Dollar*, p. 147.
[14]*Ibid.*, p. 43.
[15]*Find a Victim*, p. 138-139.
[16]*Black Money*, p. 518.
[17]*The Wycherly Woman*, p. 65.
[18]*The Zebra-Striped Hearse*, p. 1.
[19]*The Doomsters*, p. 124.
[20]*The Drowning Pool*, p. 21.
[21]*The Underground Man*, p. 65.
[22]*Ibid.*, p. 205.
[23]*The Wycherly Woman*, p. 187.
[24]*Sleeping Beauty*, p. 1.
[25]*Ibid.*, p. 2.
[26]*Ibid.*, p. 109.
[27]*Ibid.*, p. 208.
[28]*The Barbarous Coast*, p. 371.
[29]*Ibid.*, p. 458.

[30]*Find a Victim*, p. 104.
[31]*The Doomsters*, p. 154.
[32]*The Zebra-Striped Hearse*, p. 208.
[33]*The Far Side of the Dollar*, p. 149.
[34]*The Goodbye Look*, p. 57.
[35]*The Underground Man*, p. 132.
[36]*The Galton Case*, p. 16
[37]*Sleeping Beauty*, p. 24-25.

Chapter XI

[1]*The Moving Target*, p. 63.
[2]*The Far Side of the Dollar*, p. 84.
[3]*Find a Victim*, p. 128.
[4]*The Wycherly Woman*, p. 128.
[5]*The Instant Enemy*, p. 90.
[6]*The Zebra-Striped Hearse*, p. 97.
[7]*The Chill*, p. 257.
[8]*Ibid.*, p. 360.
[9]*The Zebra-Striped Hearse*, p. 136.
[10]*Black Money*, p. 577.
[11]*The Far Side of the Dollar*, p. 197.
[12]*Ibid.*, p. 5.
[13]*Ibid.*, p. 40.
[14]*The Goodbye Look*, p. 12.
[15]*The Doomsters*, p. 122.
[16]*The Galton Case*, p. 124.
[17]*The Barbarous Coast*, p. 391.
[18]*Black Money*, p. 513.
[19]*Ibid.*, p. 601.
[20]*The Chill*, p. 261.
[21]*The Blue Hammer*, p. 130.

Chapter XII

[1]*The Galton Case*, p. 173.
[2]"Gone Girl," p. 17.
[3]*The Barbarous Coast*, p. 490.
[4]*The Zebra-Striped Hearse*, p. 182.
[5]*Ibid.*, p. 216.
[6]*The Galton Case*, p. 43
[7]*Ibid.*, p. 77.
[8]*Ibid.*, p. 113.
[9]*Black Money*, p. 499.
[10]*Ibid.*, p. 539.
[11]*Ibid.*, p. 545.
[12]*The Far Side of the Dollar*, p. 12.
[13]*Ibid.*, p. 132.
[14]*Ibid.*, p. 171.
[15]*Ibid.*, p. 154.
[16]*The Goodbye Look*, p. 17.
[17]*The Instant Enemy*, p. 176.
[18]*The Underground Man*, p. 150.
[19]*The Blue Hammer*, p. 3.
[20]*Ibid.*, p. 25.
[21]*Ibid.*, p. 147.
[22]Henri J. Nouwen, in *The Wounded Healer: Ministry in Contemporary Society*. New York: Doubleday, 1979, p. 45.
[23]Sam, Grogg, Jr. "Ross Macdonald: At the Edge," in *Journal of Popular Culture* 7 (Summer, 1973): 219.

A ROSS MACDONALD BIBLIOGRAPHY

THE LEW ARCHER NOVELS
(*as* Ross Macdonald, *except where noted*)

The Moving Target [as John Macdonald]. New York: Knopf, 1949; London: Cassell, 1951; as *Harper*, New York: Pocket Books, 1966.

The Drowning Pool [as John Ross Macdonald. New York: Knopf, 1950; [as John Macdonald], London: Cassell, 1952.

The Way Some People Die [as John Ross Macdonald]. New York: Knopf, 1951; London: Cassell, 1953.

The Ivory Grin [as John Ross Macdonald]. New York: Knopf, 1952; London: Cassell,1953; as *Marked for Murder*, New York: Pocket Books, 1953.

Find A Victim [as John Ross Macdonald]. New York: Knopf, 1954; London: Cassell, 1955.

The Barbarous Coast [as John Ross Macdonald]. New York: Knopf, 1956, London: Cassell, 1957.

The Doomsters [as John Ross Macdonald]. New York: Knopf, 1958; London: Cassell, 1958.

The Galton Case [as John Ross Macdonald]. New York: Knopf, 1959, London: Cassell, 1960.

The Wycherly Woman. New York: Knopf, 1961, London: Collins, 1962.

The Zebra-Striped Hearse. New York: Knopf, 1962, London: Collins, 1963.

The Chill. New York: Knopf, and London: Collins, 1964.

The Far Side of the Dollar. New York: Knopf, and London: Collins, 1965.

Black Money. New York: Knopf, and London: Collins, 1966.

The Instant Enemy. New York: Knopf, and London: Collins, 1968.

The Goodbye Look. New York: Knopf, and London: Collins, 1969.

The Underground Man. New York: Knopf, and London: Collins, 1971.

Sleeping Beauty. New York: Knopf, London: Collins, 1973.

The Blue Hammer. New York: Knopf, London: Collins, 1976.

SHORT STORY COLLECTIONS
(*featuring* LEW ARCHER)

The Name Is Archer [as John Ross Macdonald]. New York: Bantam, 1955.

Archer in Hollywood. New York: Alferd A. Knopf, 1967.

Archer at Large. New York: Alfred A. Knopf, 1970.

Lew Archer, Private Investigator. Yonkers, New York: Mysterious Press, 1977.

OTHER CRIME PUBLICATIONS
(*which do not feature* Lew Archer)

Find the Woman. New York: Maiden Murders, 1952.

Meet Me at the Morgue [as John Ross Macdonald]. New York: Knopf, 1953; as *Experience with Evil*, London: Cassell, 1954.
The Ferguson Affair. New York: Knopf, 1960; London: Collins, 1961.
Great Stories of Suspense (anthology, as editor). New York: Alfred A. Knopf, 1974.

THE NOVELS OF KENNETH MILLAR
(featuring series character: CHET GORDON*)*

The Dark Tunnel. New York: Dodd, Mead, 1944; as *I Die Slowly*, London: Lion, 1955.
Trouble Follows Me. New York: Dodd, Mead, 1946; as *Night Train*, London: Lion, 1955.

*(*KENNETH MILLAR *novels, no series character)*

Blue City. New York: Knopf, 1947; London: Cassell, 1949.
The Three Roads. New York: Knopf, 1948; London: Cassell, 1950.

SHORT STORIES

"Shock Treatment" (as Kenneth Millar), in *Manhunt* (New York), January 1953.
"The Imaginary Blonde" (as John Ross Macdonald), in *Manhunt* (New York), February 1953.
"The Guilty One" (as John Ross Macdonald), in *Manhunt* (New York), May 1953.
"The Beat-Up Sister" (as John Ross Macdonald), in *Manhunt* (New York), October 1953.
"Murder Is a Public Matter," in *Ellery Queen's Mystery Magazine* (New York), September 1959.
"Bring the Killer to Justice," in *Ellery Queen's Mystery Magazine* (New York), February 1962.
"Bad Blood" (as John Ross Macdonald), in *Manhunt* (New York), April-May, 1967
"The Singing Pigeon," in *Alfred Hitchcock Presents: A Month of Mystery*. New York: Random House, 1969.
"The Missing Sister Case," in *Ellery Queen's Champions of Mystery*. New York: Davis, 1977; London: Gollancz, 1978.

NON-FICTION

"A Death Road for the Condor," in *Sports Illustrated*, 1964.
"Homage to Dashiell Hammettt," in *Mystery Writers' Annual*, 1964.
"Life with the Blob," in *Sports Illustrated*, 1969.
"Foreword," in *Black Tide*, by Robert Easton. New York: Delacorte Press, 1972.
On Crime Writing. Santa Barbara, California: Capra Press, 1973
A Collection of Reviews. Northridge, California: Lord John Press, 1980.
Self-Portrait: Ceaselessly into the Past, ed. by Ralph Sipper. Santa Barbara, California: Capra Press, 1981.

MARY S. WEINKAUF

SELECTED SECONDARY SOURCES

Babener, Liahna. "California Babylon: The World of American Detective Fiction," in *Clues* 1 (Fall/Winter, 1980): 77-89.

Barnes, Daniel R. "'I'm The Eye': Archer as Narrator in The Novels of Ross Macdonald," in *The Mystery and Detection Annual*, edited by Donald K. Adams. Beverly Hills, California: The Castle Press, 1972, p. 178-190.

Brown, Russell. "Ross Macdonald as Canadian Mystery Writer," in *Seasoned Authors for a New Season*, edited by Louis Filler. Bowling Green, Ohio: Bowling Green State University Popular Press, 1980, p. 164-169.

Brucolli, Matthew J. *Kenneth Millar/Ross Macdonald: A Descriptive Bibliography.* Pittsburgh: University of Pittsburgh Press, 1983.

Carlson, Arnold E. *The Living God.* St. Peter, MN: Gustavus Adolphus Press, 1951.

Evans, T. Jess. "Robert Parker and the Hardboiled Tradition of American Detective Fiction," in *Clues* 1 (Fall/Winter, 1980): 100-108.

Forell, George W. *The Ausburg Confession: A Contemporary Commentary.* Minneapolis: Ausburg, 1968.

Geherin, David. *Sons of Sam Spade: The Private-Eye Novel in the 70s.* New York: Frederick Ungar, 1980.

Grella, George. "Murder and the Mean Streets," in *Detective Fiction: Crime and Compromise*, edited by Dick Allen and David Chacko. New York: Harcourt Brace Jovanovich, 1974, p. 411-428.

Grogg, Sam, Jr. "Ross Macdonald: At the Edge," in *Journal of Popular Culture.* 7 (Summer, 1973): 213-232.

Grossvogel, David I. *Mystery and Its Fictions.* Baltimore and London: Johns Hopkins, 1979.

Harper, Ralph. *The World of the Thriller.* Cleveland: Case Western Reserve, 1969.

Hartman, Geoffrey H. "Literature High and Low: The Case of the Mystery Story," in *The Fate of Reading and Other Essays.* Chicago: University of Chicago Press, 1976, p. 203-222.

Johnson, Gib. "Heroes of Whodunits," in *West Coast Review of Books* 6 (September, 1980): 12-16.

Kenneth Millar/Ross Macdonald—A Checklist. Detroit, MI: Gale Research Co., 1971.

Lang, Betsy. "The Eligible List," in *Murderess Ink*, edited by Dilys Winn. New York: Workman Publishing, 1979, p. 169-170.

Lingeman, Richard R. "How to Tell Spade from Marlowe from Archer," in *Murder Ink*, edited by Dilys Winn. New York: Workman, 1977, p. 126-131.

Macdonald, Ross. "Down These Streets a Mean Man Must Go," in *Antaeus* (Spring/Summer, 1977).

———. "Homage to Dashiell Hammett," in *Mystery Writers' Annual*, 1964.

———. *In the First Person* [from the Davidson Films shooting script, 1971].

_____. "Place in Fiction," in *South Dakota Review* 13 (Autumn, 1975): ix, 83-84.

_____. *Self-Portrait: Ceaselessly Into the Past.* Santa Barbara, California: Capra Press, 1981.

_____. "The Writer as Detective Hero," in *On Crime Writing.* Santa Barbara, California: Capra Press, 1973.

_____. "Writing the Galton Case," in *On Crime Writing.* Santa Barbara, California: Capra Press, 1973.

Nouwen, Henri J. *The Wounded Healer: Ministry in Contemporary Society.* New York: Doubleday, 1979.

Palmer, Jerry. *Thrillers: Genesis and Structure of a Popular Genre.* New York: St. Martin's Press, 1974.

Parker, Robert B. *The Violent Hero, Wilderness Heritage and Urban Reality: A Study of the Private Eye in the Novels of Dashiell Hammett, Raymond Chandler and Ross Macdonald.* Unpublished doctoral dissertation.

Paterson, John. "A Cosmic View of the Private Eye," in *The Saturday Review* (August 22, 1953): 7-8, 31-33.

Ruehlmann, William. *Saint With a Gun: The Unlawful American Private Eye.* New York: New York University Press, 1974.

Simms, L. Moody, Jr. "Kenneth Millar/Ross Macdonald, Frank Norris, and Popular Literature," in *North Dakota Quarterly* 49 (Winter, 1981): 89-90.

Sipper, Ralph B. "An Interview with Ross Macdonald," in *Mystery and Detection Annual*, 1973.

Sokolov, Raymond, "The Art of Murder," in *Newsweek* (March 22, 1971): 101-108.

Speir, Jerry. *Ross Macdonald.* New York: Frederick Ungar Publishing Co., 1978.

Symons, Julian. *Mortal Consequences.* New York: Schocken Books, 1973.

Welty, Eudora. "Ross Macdonald's *The Underground Man*," in *The Eye of the Story.* New York: Random House, 1977, p. 251-260.

Wolfe, Peter. *Dreamers Who Live Their Dreams: The World of Ross Macdonald's Novels.* Bowling Green, Ohio: Popular Press, 1976.

INDEX

Title Index

Character Index